Using Behavioral
Objectives in the
Classroom

My chief desire . . .
is to secure the opportunity
to perfect myself
in the art of teaching.
                    —Louis Pasteur

Using Behavioral Objectives in the Classroom

Daniel Tanner
Rutgers University

The Macmillan Company, New York
Collier-Macmillan Limited, London

To Bernie and Ellie

THE MACMILLAN COMPANY
866 THIRD AVENUE, NEW YORK, NEW YORK 10022

COLLIER-MACMILLAN CANADA, LTD., TORONTO, ONTARIO

Library of Congress catalog card number: 72–77656

Printing: 1 2 3 4 5 6 7 8   Year: 2 3 4 5 6 7 8

Preface

This book is designed for teachers and prospective teachers; its aim is to help them to make use of a broad spectrum of instructional objectives and to assess learning outcomes more effectively through teacher-constructed tests. The focus is not merely on the assessment of student achievement, but on the use of teacher-made tests to improve the teaching-learning process by stimulating students to become engaged in a wide range of cognitive and affective processes.

In recent years unprecedented attention has been given to behavioral objectives as a result of developments in instructional technology and programmed instruction, along with the growing concern for improving educational efficiency through "accountability" and for assessing student achievement in various curriculum projects. A great many of these efforts have been guided by an ultraoperationalist rationale, with the result that the specificity demanded of the learner has led educators to concentrate mainly on the lower cognitive skills. As a result, many of the higher cognitive processes have been neglected while, at the same time, what Dewey called collateral learning has been ignored almost completely. Moreover, insufficient attention has been given to the necessary interdependence and continuity between affective and cognitive processes in classroom teaching and learning. The tendency has been to regard information as knowledge and to treat such "knowledge" as products or ends rather than as means or resources for reflective thinking and continued learning.

"Knowledge does not keep any better than fish," commented Whitehead almost half a century ago. Here Whitehead was not merely referring to the great changes in knowledge as a result of the twentieth-century knowledge explosion, but to the tendency for teachers to treat knowledge as something that is to be "pocketed" rather than as the means of making more comprehensible the "new world of new times."

In this book, attention also is given to the limitations of paper-and-pencil tests in assessing behavioral objectives and outcomes in the classroom. Although many proponents of behavioral objectives speak of the need to build instructional specifications so as to induce "terminal" behaviors, the position taken throughout this book is that learning is not a terminal process and that knowledge is not an end product of education but the resource for further learning by the autonomous individual. The goal of education is not to control the learner, but to enable the learner to control his own learning.

Although this book is divided into two parts, with Part I focusing on cognitive objectives and outcomes and Part II on affective objectives and outcomes, emphasis is given throughout Parts I and II to the vital interdependence and continuity between cognitive and affective processes. In both Parts I and II illustrative items in a variety of teaching fields are presented to serve as practical models for teachers in constructing tests and learning exercises that represent a wide spectrum of cognitive and affective processes. The illustrative items are related to an appropriate "taxonomy" of educational objectives. The purpose is to enable practicing and prospective teachers to understand how the items are geared to various cognitive and affective levels and to make use of the models provided in devising their own techniques.

The problems and bibliographies at the end of Parts I and II are intended to stimulate readers to examine further some of the major issues discussed in the book and to investigate additional sources.

It is hoped that this book will serve as a practical guide for practicing and prospective teachers not only in improving the teaching-learning process, but in reaching a fuller and richer understanding of the problems and issues underlying the uses of instructional objectives in the classroom.

Daniel Tanner

Contents

Part I

Instructional Goals and Outcomes —Cognitive Objectives

" 'Knowing' the definitions, rules, formulae, etc., is like knowing the names of parts of a machine without knowing what they do," observed Dewey.[1] Here Dewey was attacking traditional schooling in which mere information is taken as knowledge and in which such information is treated didactically by the teacher, only to be learned by rote and reproduced on the examination paper by the student. Because such information is not based upon understanding and interpretation, and because it does not involve application in a variety of new situations, it is readily forgotten.

To Dewey, knowledge is not merely a state of consciousness, but consists of what we consciously do or make use of in understanding what is happening, in "straightening out a perplexity, by conceiving the connection between ourselves and the world in which we live." [2] If we accept Dewey's conception of knowledge, then much of what is taught in the classroom and tested for in teacher-made achievement tests is not knowledge, but mere information. Memorization and regurgitation of information does not, in and of itself, enable us to understand and improve our environment anymore than the computer can improve its own environment through its capacity to store and retrieve information. Indeed, the computer is far more efficient than the human learner in storing and retrieving data. If the learner is to conceive the connection between himself and the world in which he lives, and if he is to function effectively in society, then he must be able to ask questions in seeking answers to problems. The computer is dependent upon man for its source of data and for the quantifiable problems to be processed. The computer thrives on repetition. Man thrives on the great variety of perplexities that he must encounter and

---

[1] John Dewey, *Democracy and Education* (New York: The Macmillan Company, 1916), p. 261.
[2] Ibid., p. 400.

solve in making his life meaningful and rewarding in an ever-changing world. This calls for a much wider vision of knowledge and learning than is evidenced in many teacher-made examinations.

Moreover, knowledge is not something that exists apart from interests, attitudes, appreciations, and values. Our feelings or emotions cannot be separated from our capacity to learn and to act thoughtfully within and upon our environment. As discussed later in this section and in Part II, man's development of new knowledge, and the uses to which such knowledge is put, is governed by interests, attitudes, appreciations, and values.

Although the main focus of Part II of this book is on affective goals and outcomes, whereas Part I is devoted primarily to cognitive goals and outcomes of classroom instruction, the necessary interdependence and continuity between cognitive and affective learning is stressed throughout both Parts I and II.

DOMAINS OF INSTRUCTIONAL OBJECTIVES

Although several investigators have sought to develop a classification system of instructional objectives, the most systematic approaches have been developed by Bloom, Krathwohl, and associates, who classified various objectives within a "taxonomic system." [3] The major purpose of the "taxonomic system" was to enable teachers, curriculum workers, and testing specialists to communicate more effectively in discerning the nature and scope of instructional goals. It was assumed that such a system would help educators to plan and evaluate learning experiences more effectively, and to compare existing curriculum goals with a wide range of possible outcomes, thereby increasing the possibilities of developing a broader spectrum of goals and outcomes. In essence, the "taxonomic system" was designed to classify the intended behavior of students as a result of participating in some set of instructional experiences, and to be used in obtaining evidence on the extent to which such behaviors are manifest.

Three Domains

Bloom, Krathwohl, and their associates developed a threefold division of instructional objectives: (1) cognitive: the recall or recognition of knowledge and the development of intellectual abilities and skills; (2) affective: changes in interests, attitudes, and values, and the development of appreciations; and (3) psychomotor: development of manipulative or motor skills. Although psychomotor objectives are dealt with in a variety of learning activities—such as handwriting, speech, typing, physical education, laboratory sciences, industrial arts, and vocational and technical education—the developers of the taxonomy noted

---

[3] Benjamin S. Bloom (ed.), *Taxonomy of Educational Objectives, Handbook I: Cognitive Domain* (New York: David McKay Company, Inc., 1956); and David R. Krathwohl, Benjamin S. Bloom, and Bertram B. Masia, *Taxonomy of Educational Objectives, Handbook II: Affective Domain* (New York: David McKay Company, Inc., 1964).

that few psychomotor objectives were to be found in the literature.[4] Consequently, they proceeded to concentrate their efforts on developing taxonomies
for the cognitive and affective domains.

Interdependence and Continuity

In constructing the taxonomies of cognitive and affective objectives, it was
acknowledged that modern behavioral science reveals that humans do not think
or behave without feeling, but respond as total organisms or as whole beings.
Nevertheless, it was decided that instructional objectives should be classified
into two separate domains, cognitive and affective, on the grounds that
"teachers and curriculum workers who state objectives do make distinctions
between problem solving and attitudes, between thinking and feeling, and
between acting and thinking or feeling." [5]

When researchers find little relationship between cognitive achievement and
attitudes or values, this does not mean that the educator need only concentrate
on cognitive goals while ignoring the affective domain. Many students will meet
the cognitive objectives expected of them in mathematics or in English literature in order to gain a suitable grade for college entrance, but they may also
learn to dislike these subjects intensively. Under such circumstances it is less
likely that they will elect to specialize in these fields in college than if, in high
school, they had developed highly favorable interests, attitudes, and appreciations in connection with these subject matters.

The developers of the taxonomies noted that "it was evident in our work
that, although one could place an objective very readily in one of the three
major domains or classes, no objective in one class was entirely devoid of some
components of the other two classes." [6] For example, the learner may be asked
to analyze the conflicting sides of a public issue on which he already has a strong
bias. In order to gain a full understanding of the viewpoints which conflict
with his own biased point of view, he must be open to the full weight of evidence in support of the opposing side. If he changes his point of view in the
light of the new evidence, then the cognitive learning that has taken place has
altered his affective posture on the issue. Reciprocally, he might not have been
able to examine the opposing evidence fully if he had allowed his bias to inter-
fere with his cognitive processes. In dealing with controversy, the interdependence of the cognitive and affective processes are most readily apparent. But
these processes are interdependent and virtually inseparable in all kinds of
situations involving human learning.

Dewey pointed to the fallacy of conceiving of the emotions as having nothing
to do with the work of intelligence in apprehending facts and truths. Dewey
emphasized the untenability of this dualism in the light of the biological con-

---

4 Krathwohl, Bloom, and Masia, op. cit., p. 7.
5 Ibid.
6 Ibid., p. 8.

tinuity of the human organism.[7] Although appreciations are distinguished from symbolic experiences, Dewey maintained that

> They [appreciations] are not to be distinguished from the work of the intellect or understanding. Only a personal response involving imagination can possibly procure realization even of pure "facts." The imagination is the medium of appreciation in every field. The engagement of the imagination is the only thing that makes any activity more than mechanical. Unfortunately, it is too customary to identify the imagination with the imaginary, rather than with warm and intimate taking in of the full scope of a situation.[8]

The interdependence of the three domains in relationship to the learner's system of needs and developmental tasks is shown schematically in Figure 1. As discussed earlier, the developers of the taxonomies of instructional objectives recognized the continuity and interdependence of the three domains but chose to treat them separately for purposes of focus and in view of the distinctions

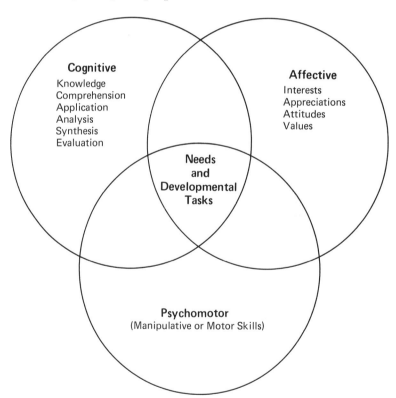

FIGURE 1. Interdependence of cognitive, affective, and psychomotor domains, and their relationship to needs and developmental tasks.

---

[7] Dewey, op. cit., pp. 390–393.
[8] Ibid., p. 276.

made in classroom instruction and in curriculum materials. Yet it should be stressed that although the term *domain* implies a separation of spheres of activity, in effective learning these spheres are marked not by separation and isolation, but by continuity and interdependence. Nevertheless, it is useful for teachers and curriculum workers to examine these so-called domains separately with a view toward (1) developing teaching–learning strategies and evaluative measures that are more fully representative of the broad spectrum of cognitive goals that are attainable, (2) developing teaching–learning strategies that are representative of affective goals relevant to the curriculum, and (3) developing needed interrelationships between cognitive and affective goals in the teaching–learning process and in the evaluation of achievement.

EVALUATION OF LEARNING OUTCOMES

"Evaluation is a two-edged sword which can enhance student learning and personality development or be destructive of student learning and personality development," observes Bloom.[9] Accordingly, educators need to determine whether examinations and other evaluative procedures "have a positive effect on student learning and instruction" and whether they "leave both teachers and students with a positive view of themselves and of the subject and learning process."[10] Consequently, the evaluation of student achievement not only can and should be a valuable part of the student's learning experiences, but can and should be a key means of providing the teacher and other curriculum workers with valuable feedback for improving the effectiveness of curriculum and instruction.

Formative and Summative Evaluation

The use of teacher-made tests for purposes of both "formative" and "summative" evaluation has received increasing attention on the part of educators in recent years. "Formative" evaluation refers to the use of tests and other evaluative procedures while the course or instructional program is in progress, whereas "summative" evaluation occurs at the end of the course, unit, or instructional program.

Feedback. Although many teachers think of formative evaluation mainly as the means of assessing individual student achievement for purposes of assigning grades, such evaluation is of crucial importance in providing the teacher and curriculum developers with continuous feedback for improving the teaching–

---

[9] Benjamin S. Bloom, "Some Theoretical Issues Relating to Educational Evaluation," Chapter 3 in *Educational Evaluation: New Roles, New Means,* Sixty-eighth Yearbook, Part II, National Society for the Study of Education (Chicago: The University of Chicago Press, 1969), p. 45.

[10] Ibid., p. 46.

learning process and the curriculum materials. Equally important in formative evaluation is the use of tests and other evaluative procedures as learning aids and as a means of providing feedback to the student concerning his progress.

Unfortunately, however, the use of tests for formative evaluation is directed by many teachers primarily, if not almost entirely, at assessing student achievement for purposes of assigning grades. Under such circumstances, the tests tend to be regarded by students as hurdles or as instruments of crisis. This leads many students, including the best students, to concentrate their time and energies on preparing for the tests rather than on pursuing aspects of the course of study that are of genuine personal interest.

Comprehensive Evaluation. The summative evaluation which occurs at the end of the course, term, or unit may also be detrimental to the teaching–learning process when student grades are determined to a great extent on the basis of scores on midterm and final examinations. Teachers would do well to develop and employ a variety of devices and procedures in evaluating student achievement—including the assessment of projects, themes, laboratory work, reports, and other assignments—in addition to examinations at both the formative and summative stages. Furthermore, summative evaluation should be employed in assessing the success of the course and in comparing alternative curricula. Such comprehensive evaluation can provide essential feedback to the teacher and curriculum worker for purposes of curriculum improvement.

"Primarily it is the schools and not the scholars which should be inspected," observed Whitehead.[11] By conceiving of formative and summative evaluation as means of ascertaining the effectiveness of the instructional program, improving the curriculum, and diagnosing ways in which students can become more successful through meaningful learning, such evaluation can serve a constructive and vital purpose. In this connection teachers would do well to subject their own tests to inspection.

Testing for Thinking

Emphasized throughout Part I of this book is the need to develop and employ teacher-made tests as tools to help the student to learn how to utilize knowledge as thought. Most of Part I focuses on the need to devise tests which encompass a wider range of cognitive processes. When students gain experiences in dealing with knowledge not as mere information and narrowly conceived skills, but as the raw material for comprehending, analyzing, synthesizing, and evaluating questions or problems of personal and social significance, they will be learning *how* to think and not merely *what* to think. Dewey noted that much of what passes for school learning as measured by examinations is either

---

[11] Alfred North Whitehead, *The Aims of Education and Other Essays* (New York: The Macmillan Company, 1929), p. 21.

forgotten or must be unlearned if the student is to move ahead intellectually in the stream of life.

> Almost everyone has had occasion to look back upon his school days and wonder what has become of the knowledge he was supposed to have amassed during his years of schooling, and why it is that the technical skills he acquired have to be learned over again in changed form in order to stand him in good stead. Indeed, he is lucky who does not find that in order to make progress, in order to go ahead intellectually, he does not have to unlearn much of what he learned in school. These questions cannot be disposed of by saying that the subjects were not actually learned, for they were learned at least sufficiently to enable a pupil to pass examinations in them.[12]

Examinations that require the student merely to memorize and regurgitate information serve as artifacts of the time-worn doctrine of mental discipline in which the mind is regarded as a muscle to be strengthened through repetitive exercise. Such learning bears virtually no connection with "reason."

"Pupils who have stored their 'minds' with all kinds of material which they have never put to intellectual uses," wrote Dewey, "are sure to be hampered when they try to think."[13] So much subject matter is forgotten because the emphasis is on "the accumulation and acquisition of information for purposes of reproduction in recitation and examination," instead of being on knowledge as "the working capital, the indispensable resources, for further inquiry."[14]

Memorized information may serve the utilitarian purpose of getting the student through the examination, but otherwise it has no utility or relevance in the life of the learner. It is painstakingly memorized and painlessly forgotten.

THE COGNITIVE DOMAIN

As mentioned earlier, Bloom, Krathwohl, and their associates developed a classification schema or taxonomy of cognitive and affective objectives in terms of the intended behaviors of students as a result of participation in some learning activity. In the cognitive domain, the behaviors are identified in terms of a range of acts of thinking.

Bloom and his associates acknowledge that the determination of the classes and their titles is somewhat arbitrary and that virtually any number of methods can be used in deciding on the categories and terminology of instructional objectives. For this reason there is doubt as to whether their classification schema is a true taxonomy in the scientific sense. Nevertheless, this does not restrict its usefulness. Teachers and curriculum workers can use the schema to develop teaching–learning strategies and evaluative devices that represent a

---

[12] John Dewey, *Experience and Education* (New York: The Macmillan Company, 1938), pp. 47–48.
[13] Dewey, *Democracy and Education,* op. cit., p. 186.
[14] Ibid.

more comprehensive representation of cognitive goals than is characteristic of traditional education.

Classification of Cognitive Objectives

The classification schema or taxonomy of cognitive objectives developed by Bloom and his associates represents an attempt to arrange instructional objectives in a hierarchical order—from simple to complex classes of thinking. Despite the hierarchical construction, they sought to avoid the view that the higher cognitive classes are necessarily more valuable. The value of a cognitive act depends upon the particular problem situation, although it is widely acknowledged that the higher or more complex cognitive levels incorporate many of the simpler cognitive abilities.

The classification schema developed by Bloom and others for the cognitive domain is summarized as follows: [15]

Cognitive Taxonomy

Knowledge

1.00 Knowledge
Recall of specifics and universals, recall of methods and processes, or recall of a pattern, structure, or setting.
  1.10 *Knowledge of Specifics*
  Recall of specific and isolable bits of information.
  1.11 *Knowledge of Terminology*
  Knowledge of the referents for specific symbols (verbal and nonverbal), such as defining technical terms and giving their attributes, or recognizing the symbols in a formula.
  1.12 *Knowledge of Specific Acts*
  Knowledge of dates, events, persons, places, sources of information, etc.
1.20 Knowledge of Ways and Means of Dealing with Specifics
Knowledge of the ways of organizing, studying, judging, and criticizing —chiefly in the awareness of systems such as sequences, standards, methods, and procedures—rather than in the ability to make use of these systems and their processes.
  1.21 *Knowledge of Conventions*
  Knowledge of characteristic ways of treating and presenting ideas and phenomena, such as forms and usage in speech and writing, symbols in maps and dictionaries, parliamentary procedure, etiquette, and so on.
  1.22 *Knowledge of Trends and Sequences*
  Knowledge of the processes, directions, and movements of phenomena in relation to time—such as sequences of events, procedures, movements, and trends.

---

[15] Adapted from Bloom et al., op. cit., pp. 201–207.

1.23 *Knowledge of Classifications and Categories*
Knowledge of classes, sets, divisions, and arrangements that are fundamental or useful for a given subject field, purpose, argument, or problem.

1.24 *Knowledge of Criteria*
Knowledge of the criteria by which facts, principles, opinions, and conduct are tested or judged.

1.25 *Knowledge of Methodology*
Knowledge of the techniques, procedures, and methods of inquiry employed in a particular field and in investigating problems and phenomena.

1.30 Knowledge of the Universals and Abstractions in a Field
Knowledge of the major schemes and patterns by which phenomena and ideas are organized, such as the theories and generalizations used in explaining phenomena and in solving problems.

1.31 *Knowledge of Principles and Generalizations*
Knowledge of abstractions used in describing, explaining, and predicting phenomena, or in determining courses of action.

1.32 *Knowledge of Theories and Structures*
Knowledge of the *body* of principles and generalizations representing a systematic view of a complex phenomenon, problem, or field.

Intellectual Abilities and Skills

2.00 Comprehension
Understanding what is being communicated in order to make use of the communication(s), through ideas and materials, without necessarily recognizing the fullest implications of the situation.

2.10 *Translation*
Comprehension of communications as paraphrased or rendered from one language or form to another, such as translating visual material to verbal representations or translating verbal material to mathematical representations.

2.20 *Interpretation*
Explanation or summarization of a communication, involving a rearrangement or a new perspective of the material.

2.30 *Extrapolation*
Extension of trends or tendencies beyond given data to ascertain implications, corollaries, and consequences, and to make predictions.

3.00 Application
Use of abstractions—such as ideas, principles, or theories—in concrete situations.

4.00 Analysis
Reduction of a communication into its components so that a hierarchy of ideas and their relationships is made explicit and clarified.

4.10 *Analysis of Elements*
Distinguishing the elements of a communication, such as facts from assumptions.

4.20   *Analysis of Relationships*
Connection and interactions between elements of a communication, such as relating information and assumptions to hypotheses.

4.30   *Analysis of Organizational Principles*
Systematic organization and structure which hold the communication together, such as the recognition of form and pattern in literary or artistic works.

5.00   Synthesis
Integration of elements to constitute a pattern, structure, or function which otherwise would not be manifest.

5.10   *Production of a Unique Communication*
Development and communication of unique ideas or experiences to others.

5.20   *Production of a Plan or Proposed Set of Operations*
Development of a plan by bringing together sets of data or specifications.

5.30   *Derivation of a Set of Abstract Relations*
Development of a schema for classifying or explaining particular data or phenomena, or the deduction of propositions and relations from a set of basic propositions or symbolic representations, such as the formulation of hypotheses or generalizations from data.

6.00   Evaluation
Judging the value of ideas, materials, procedures, or methods according to criteria or standards.

6.10   *Judgments in Terms of Internal Evidence*
Evaluation of a situation through such evidence as logical accuracy, consistency, and validity.

6.20   *Judgments in Terms of External Criteria*
Evaluation of a situation with reference to selected criteria, such as comparing a work against the highest known standards in its field.

THE COGNITIVE TAXONOMY: ILLUSTRATIVE ITEMS

Teacher-made tests of the paper-and-pencil variety constitute only one of many devices and procedures in evaluating learning outcomes. As discussed earlier, teachers also evaluate student themes, laboratory work, projects, oral reports, homework assignments, recitations, and so on. However, in most of the "academic" subjects in the secondary school, the paper-and-pencil test, particularly the so-called objective test, is perhaps the most dominant single device for assessing student achievement.

Ironically, in life one would not measure the worth of a scientist, engineer, baker, lawyer, welder, artist, physician, or plumber according to his performance on a paper-and-pencil test. Nevertheless, in most occupations which require licensing, written examinations are used as an important device for establishing and assessing minimum achievement standards for entry. Because the school is necessarily concerned with achievement standards, a great deal of time and effort is devoted to paper-and-pencil testing. Obviously, such tests can be useful in diagnosing certain learning outcomes, ascertaining particular strengths and needs of the learner, clarifying curriculum objectives, and promoting specific types of learning.

Unfortunately, however, tests often are badly constructed, with their use being largely limited to measuring the mere recall of information, whereby knowledge is represented in the most artificial of contexts. The educational problem is not to abolish paper-and-pencil tests, but to use them more effectively for measuring and bringing about more significant and authentic learning outcomes. Such tests must be used as only one of many devices and procedures for evaluating and stimulating desirable learning outcomes.

In this section several test items are offered to illustrate a range of cognitive objectives which can be sought by the teacher and learner in a variety of subject fields. The purpose is not to provide an exhaustive treatment of cognitive objectives, but rather to illustrate how some items can be constructed to represent a range of thought processes.

Sample Test Items—Lower Cognitive Levels

Earlier it was noted that the most common educational objective in traditional classroom instruction is the recall or acquisition of information. The following item is taken from an actual teacher-made test:

> The *Scarlet Letter* was written in the year _____.

The preceding item is limited to the mere recall of a specific and isolated piece of information or fact, placing it at the lowest level of the cognitive taxonomy. However, the fact that it is at the lowest level of the cognitive taxonomy does not in itself make it an undesirable test item. What makes it undesirable is that it requires the learner to recall a specific fact or piece of information in the absence of stimulating the learner to demonstrate some understanding of the significance of the fact. Unless facts or information are placed in a contextual relationship or put to use, such material is apt to be meaningless, and because it is meaningless, it is simply memorized for the examination and promptly forgotten by sensible students.

Ways and Means of Dealing with Specifics. If the purpose of the preceding item is to evaluate the learner's ability to relate specific literary works to various time periods, this can be accomplished without the necessity of requiring him to memorize specific dates. For example, the assessment of the learner's sense of time in connection with specific literary works might be approached through the following item:

> *Directions:* Place the following five literary works in the blanks above the time line in the order in which these works appeared.

The Grapes of Wrath
The Red Badge of Courage
The Scarlet Letter
Animal Farm
An American Tragedy

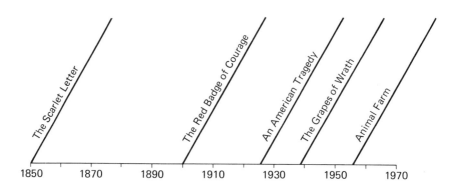

The preceding item requires the student to deal with specifics by placing them in a time sequence. Simple memorization of dates is not necessary. It is somewhat higher on the cognitive taxonomy than the first item because it assesses the student's ability to deal with specifics rather than merely to recall specifics. The teacher may wish to follow this item with related questions in which the student is asked to identify the authors of the given works (recalling specifics); connect specific works to historic events or eras (relating specifics to sequences); connect specific works to literary themes, styles, and movements (relating specifics to conventions and sequences); and so on.

Sample Test Items—Higher Cognitive Levels

At considerably higher cognitive levels are items that require the student to *comprehend* (*interpret* and *extrapolate*), and *analyze* material from given sources of data, such as a literary passage.

> *Directions:* Below is a passage from a novel. After reading the passage, answer the questions which follow.
>
> He felt a quiet manhood, non-assertive but of sturdy and strong blood. . . . He had been to touch the great death, and found that, after all, it was but the great death. He was a man.
> So it came to pass as he trudged from the place of blood and wrath his soul changed. He came from hot plowshares to prospects of clover tranquility, and it was as if hot plowshares were not. Scars faded as flowers.
>
> 1. The novel from which the above passage is taken is The Red Badge of Courage.
> 2. The author of the above novel is Stephen Crane.

3. The theme which best represents the above passage is
  _____a. an old man's reminiscences of his war experiences as a youth.
  _____b. the horrors of war.
  _____c. a youth gaining manhood from football.
  _____d. a youth gaining peace and manhood through religious con-
  version.
  __x__ e. a youth gaining manhood in war.
4. The novel from which the passage was taken was written about
  _____a. Vietnam.
  _____b. contemporary college football.
  _____c. World War II.
  _____d. the Revolutionry War.
  __x__ e. the Civil War.

Short essay-type items can be useful in enriching and extending the range of cognitive levels and styles in which the student can become engaged. However, the teacher should be clear as to the criteria by which the student answers are to be evaluated while, at the same time, being open to unexpected and unique insights. The following is one example of a highly specific essay-type item which requires the student to engage in *comprehension (translation, interpretation, extrapolation), application* of specifics to general ideas or themes, *analysis* of relationships, and also possibly *synthesis* of certain elements into a unifying theme or message:

In what respects (how and why) is each of the following titles significant in representing the major theme or meaning of each novel:

a. *For Whom the Bell Tolls.*
b. *The Red Badge of Courage.*
c. *The Grapes of Wrath.*
d. *An American Tragedy.*
e. *The Scarlet Letter.*

An essay-type item, presented below, requires the student to *apply* his knowledge of history in *analyzing* a given statement and supporting a given conclusion:

According to the 1969 report of the National Commission on the Causes and Prevention of Violence, "the U.S. is the clear leader among modern, stable democratic nations in its rates of homicide, assault, rape, robbery, and it is at least among the highest in incidence of group violence and assassination." James Truslow Adams observed that "lawlessness has been and is one of the most distinctive American traits."

From your knowledge of American history, what events can you cite to support Adams' belief that "lawlessness has been one of the most distinctive American traits"?

An essay item that is carefully structured but that, at the same time, allows the student to produce a unique communication (*synthesis*) is illustrated as follows:

Directions: Below are two accounts of an event presented in very different styles. After reading the two accounts, reconstruct the event in the style of a scene from a *play.*

Newspaper

Nutley, N.J., Dec. 24. Postmaster Ambrose J. Hazard declared today that at least 30 per cent of the mailmen in Nutley, N.J. had been treated for canine attacks of some sort during the past two months. Interviewed at the Nutley General Hospital, Hazard warned that persons who fail to curb their dogs may be required to pick up their own mail at the post office.

St. Bernard owner David O. Gristle, who was visiting one of the victims at Nutley General Hospital contended that "A dog will only attack a vicious human being."

In a city-wide survey conducted by *The Nutley Intelligentsia,* it was found that 45 per cent of the residents held that the mailmen were to blame for provoking the attacks, 38 per cent blamed the dog owners, 5 per cent blamed the dogs, and 12 per cent were undecided.

Mayor John V. Glibly stated that a compromise must be worked out.

Bible

And it came about in the land of Nutley that many dogs attacked the sons of Nutley.

And there was in the land of Nutley a righteous man, Ambrose. And Ambrose was the son of Isaiah. And Isaiah was the son of Gabriel. And Gabriel was the son of Ishmael, born in the great wilderness.

Now it had come to pass that because of the evil of the tribe of Nutley, they were attacked by many dogs.

And so Ambrose did say to the elders of Nutley, "Go and speak the truth to all men that evil hath come to our tribe. Do ye no evil that these dogs and sons of dogs shall no longer plague us."

And David, the son of Gristle, did say, "Ambrose did speak the truth. For it is commanded that evil be punished. Be ye kind to one another as ye are kind to animals."

And the city elder, John, did bless them all.

The following items from another subject field (biology) require the student to engage in the processes of *interpretation* and *extrapolation* by *analyzing* given information or data; at the same time, the student must demonstrate some background knowledge in order to answer the items correctly:

Below is a quotation from an actual letter written by a scientist to a fellow scientist.

I do not know whether the records of British Surgery ever meet your eye. If so, you will have seen from time to time notices of the antiseptic system of treatment, which I have been labouring for the last nine years to bring to perfection.

Allow me to take this opportunity to tender you my most cordial thanks for having, by your brilliant researches, demonstrated to me the truth of the germ theory of putrefaction, and thus furnished me with the principle upon which alone the antiseptic system can be carried out. Should you at any time visit Edinburgh it would, I believe, give you sincere gratification to see at our hospital how largely mankind is being benefited by your labours.

I need hardly add that it would afford me the highest gratification to show you how greatly surgery is indebted to you.

1. The person to whom the above letter was addressed was <u>Louis Pasteur.</u>
2. The author of the letter was <u>Joseph Lister.</u>
3. The letter was most likely written around the year (check the answer which applies):
   _____a. 1700.
   _____b. 1775.
   __x__ c. 1875.
   _____d. 1925.
   _____e. 1970.
4. The principle referred to in the letter is based upon the
   _____a. spontaneous generation theory.
   _____b. organismic theory.
   _____c. genetic continuity theory.
   __x__ d. theory that microbes are associated with diseases of larger organisms.
   _____e. contagion theory of disease.
5. The author of the letter expressed his debt for his colleague's research which most likely was related to the hypothesis that
   _____a. man is a carrier of disease.
   _____b. viruses are carried in air.
   _____c. harmful microorganisms are easily transmitted.
   _____d. the septic property of the atmosphere is derived from oxygen.
   __x__ e. harmful microorganisms are carried in the atmosphere.
6. The author of the letter evidently has applied another scientist's discovery to the development of
   _____a. new surgical techniques.
   _____b. methods of preventing the spread of disease among surgical patients.
   _____c. methods of rendering surgical patients immune from harmful microorganisms.
   __x__ d. methods of destroying and preventing harmful microorganisms from entering the wounds of surgical patients.
   _____e. methods of keeping harmful microorganisms from entering the hospital operating room.
7. The scientist to whom the above letter was sent was most likely a
   __x__ a. bacteriologist.
   _____b. biophysicist.
   _____c. paleontologist.
   _____d. cytologist.
   _____e. taxonomist.

Items 4, 5 and 6 also require the student to *extrapolate* conclusions and generalizations from given data while demonstrating some *knowledge of universals and abstractions* in a field. Item 7 is concerned with *knowledge of classifications and categories* without requiring the student merely to give a definition. Instead the student must interpret the classification in a situation requiring *application*.

In the sciences and mathematics the traditional practice has been for students to memorize formulas and to solve test problems by plugging into the formulas the given values so as to calculate the unknown. The student is merely required to demonstrate his powers of *recall of information* and his ability to perform the mathematical computations required in the formula. Under such circumstances the student can obtain correct answers without really understanding the formula as a statement of lawful relationships. However, if the student does not fully understand the formula, he is more apt to be vulnerable to errors in calculation and he is less likely to be able to transfer what he has learned to new situations.

The curriculum reforms in the sciences and mathematics have emphasized the need to understand formulas as lawful statements and the ability to develop and use such formulas in a variety of contexts so as to improve the possibilities for transfer. The following item requires the student to demonstrate his *comprehension* of a mathematical concept by *interpreting* the concept as an expression of relationship between two variables:

> The ancient Greeks denoted the value of π as approximately 3.1416. What *relationship* does 3.1416 represent?

Here the student is expected to explain that 3.1416 represents the ratio of the circumference of any circle to its diameter. In other words, the circumference of a circle of any size is slightly more than three times its diameter. If the student understands this principle (*comprehension*), he will immediately recognize the error in the item below which presents the same concept in a situation calling for *application*.

> Joe measured the circumference of a gear and found it to be 60 inches. He then calculated the diameter of the gear as 30 inches. Assuming that Joe measured the circumference of the gear correctly, why would his calculation of the gear's diameter have to be incorrect?

The following items require the student to perform certain mathematical operations which may be classified cognitively as *extrapolation* and *analysis*:

Homicides in New York City

Year	Homicides	Rate per 100,000
1943	225	3.0
1960	385	4.9
1965	645	8.1
1970	1,146	14.6

Source: The New York Times *(March 28, 1971), p. 61.*

1. In 1970 the population of New York City was _____, as compared with _____ in 1960.

2. From 1960 to 1970 the number of homicides increased by _____ per cent.

3. Assuming that the population of New York City in 1980 will be the same as it was in 1970, and assuming that the homicide rate will rise to 24 per 100,000 in 1980, how many homicides will there be in New York City in 1980? _____.

Every teacher has encountered situations where students exhibit a greater interest in the collateral aspects of a lesson than in the target material as conceived by the teacher. Thus, for example, when mathematics is applied to social problems, such as crime and corrections, the students may become more interested in learning about the causes, consequences, and prospects of dealing with rising crime rates than in learning the mathematical operations required in the preceding items. Nevertheless, even though the teacher may not want to "stray" from the target subject matter, by enabling the student to make use of concepts and skills in different contexts, the student learns that a given subject matter has relevance to other subjects. Some implications of collateral or concommitant learning are discussed later.

In the social studies there has been a traditional tendency on the part of some teachers merely to require students to recall factual information and to memorize dates in connection with given events. Again this type of learning not only is quickly forgotten, but is not very meaningful to the student. The following items illustrate how the student might be required to relate statements to significant historical figures, events, or works, thereby engaging the student in a broader spectrum of cognitive styles:

Directions: Select the item in the key below which best fits each of the following historical quotations.

Key: a. U.S. Supreme Court Decision of 1954.
b. Dwight D. Eisenhower.
c. Franklin Delano Roosevelt.
d. *An American Dilemma.*
e. Harry S Truman.

d 1. "The bright side is that the conquering of color caste in America is America's own innermost desire. This nation early laid down as the moral basis for its existence the principles of equality and liberty. However much Americans have dodged this conviction, they have refused to adjust their laws to their own license. . . . In this sense the Negro problem is not only America's greatest failure but also America's incomparably great opportunity for the future." [16]

e 2. "There shall be a loyalty investigation of every person entering the civilian employment of any department or agency of the Executive Branch of the Federal Government."

a 3. "To separate them from others of similar age and qualifications solely because of their race generates a feeling of inferiority as to their

[16] Gunnar Myrdal, *An American Dilemma* (New York: Harper & Row, Publishers, 1944), p. 1021.

status in the community that may affect their hearts and minds in a way unlikely ever to be undone."

b 4. "In the councils of government, we must guard against the acquisition of unwarranted influence, whether sought or unsought, by the military-industrial complex. The potential for the disastrous rise of misplaced power exists and will persist. We must never let the weight of this combination endanger our liberties or democratic processes."

c 5. "In the future days, which we seek to make secure, we look forward to a world founded upon four essential human freedoms. The first is freedom of speech and expression—everywhere in the world. The second is freedom of every person to worship God in his own way —everywhere in the world. The third is freedon from want . . . —everywhere in the world. The fourth is freedom from fear— which . . . means a world-wide reduction of armaments to such a point and in such a thorough fashion that no nation will be in a position to commit an act of physical aggression against any neighbor —anywhere in the world."

e 6. "We do live in perilous times. There never was a time in the history of the world when leadership is so necessary. There never was a time in the history of the world when a moral awakening is so necessary. There never was a time in the history of the world when it becomes your duty and mine to see that the Charter of the United Nations is implemented as the law of the land and the law of the world."

The preceding items call for the cognitive skills of *interpretation, extrapolation,* and *analysis,* along with some knowledge of the *ways and means of dealing with specifics.* This series of items, in turn, might be followed by a related short-answer item requiring the student to formulate four issues in contemporary American life that are related to the preceding quotations. The short-answer item would require the student not only to extend his *analyses* of the quotations, but to *synthesize* certain quotations as issues that are applicable to the contemporary scene. For example, an issue related to the concepts of arms control, national sovereignty, security, and international peace could be developed from items 4, 5, and 6, whereas an issue related to the concepts of freedom, equality, loyalty, brotherhood of man, and racial injustice could be developed from items 1, 2, 3, and 5.

The following is an example of a short essay item that requires the student to *synthesize* several concepts by organizing them into a meaningful relationship:

Directions: In a single paragraph, use the following concepts in a meaningful relationship:

due process	law and order
equal opportunity	property rights
racial discrimination	freedom of speech

Although the student is given considerable latitude in developing his answer to the preceding item, the social studies teacher should have little difficulty in evaluating the various student responses, because the criterion for evaluation is clearly identified in the item—the degree to which the student is able to organize the concepts into a meaningful relationship in a paragraph. Yet the student is free to organize these concepts to produce a unique communication provided he is so capable.

An item likely to be of interest to adolescent boys illustrates how an important principle in a given field, physics, can be applied in a seemingly far-removed situation.

> A physicist contends that Olympic athlete A who heaves a 16-pound shot 66 feet, 11 inches in Boston actually has made a better performance than Olympic athlete B who heaves the 16-pound shot 67 feet in Acapulco. Yet the Olympic record books will credit athlete A with the better record. What is the physical principle upon which the physicist's argument is based?

Here the student is expected to explain that the gravitational force (g) differs according to latitude, and that because the gravitational force in Boston is greater than that in Acapulco, athlete A was up against a higher value of g than athlete B. In this item the student is required to *analyze* the data and make an evaluation in terms of an external criterion.

The following essay item requires the student to *evaluate* a general statement relating to a specific concept ("standard of living") after *analyzing* and *synthesizing* a set of specific data not ordinarily associated with the concept.

> It is often said that Americans enjoy the world's highest standard of living. After examining the data in the table below, criticize or defend the proposition that American's enjoy the highest standard of living in the world. (Be sure to discuss the various *criteria* through which "standard of living" may be judged, including criteria not presented in the table.)

Standard Health Indexes for Selected Industrialized Nations

	Health Index		
Nation	Life Expectancy (yrs.)		Infant Mortality (per 1,000 live births)
	Males	Females	
Sweden	71.6	75.7	12.7
Norway	71.3	75.6	12.8
Netherlands	71.1	75.9	13.5
Denmark	70.3	74.6	15.7
Switzerland	68.7	74.1	16.1
United Kingdom	68.3	74.4	18.3
France	68.0	75.1	20.4
Japan	67.7	73.0	14.9
United States	66.8	73.7	22.7

Source: *Demographic Yearbook* (New York: United Nations, Dept. of Economic and Social Affairs, 1967), and Irving J. Lewis, "Government Investment in Health Care," *Scientific American,* Vol. 224 (April, 1971), p. 19.

In the preceding item the student is required to *evaluate* a proposition after *analyzing* and *synthesizing* certain data. Although students are allowed to reach different conclusions, they must support their judgments with specific criteria. The item may stimulate one student to think divergently in his response by attacking the orthodox notions of "standard of living," whereas another student may respond convergently by supporting the validity of certain traditional notions. Nevertheless, it would be possible for both students to make equally perfect scores on the item, provided that they *evaluate* the statement according to the various criteria that can be adjudged relevant to the concept in question.

Although the following items can be organized in multiple-choice fashion, they are presented as a series of brief essay questions in order to convey to the learner the spirit of inquiry in which a scientist is engaged.

> The following quotation is taken from an actual journal article published in the year 1772:
>
> > . . . on the 17th of August, 1771, I put a sprig of mint (plant) in a quantity of air in which a wax candle had burned out, and found that on the 27th of the same month another candle had burned perfectly well in it. This experiment I repeated, without the least variation in the event, not less than eight or ten times in the remainder of the summer. Several times I divided the quantity of air in which the candle had burned out, into two parts, and putting the plant into one of them, left the other in the same exposure, contained, also, in a glass vessel immersed in water, but without any plant, and never failed to find that a candle would burn in the former but not in the latter.
>
> 1. What is the *problem* being investigated in the above experiment? (Define the *problem* as clearly and briefly as you can.)
> 2. What *hypothesis* might have guided the experiment?
> 3. What was the *control* in the above experiment? Why was this *control* used?
> 4. Why did the scientist repeat the experiment several times?
> 5. What *conclusion*(s) could be reached from the experiment?
> 6. What *evidence* can you cite from the experiment to support your conclusion(s)?
> 7. What new hypotheses might be derived as a result of the findings from the experiment? (Formulate at least one hypothesis.)
> 8. What new discoveries came about as a result of the experiment and how were these discoveries related to the experiment?

The preceding items, although simply stated, require the student to engage in a wide range of cognitive skills, such as to *interpret a sequence of events;* to exhibit some understanding of *methodology, abstractions,* and *universals* in a field; to *extrapolate* implications and consequences from given data; to *analyze* certain elements, relationships, and principles from given data; to *synthesize* certain elements into new relations; and to *evaluate* evidence. The various items require the student not only to explain *what* has occurred, but *how* and *why* certain phenomena occur in relation to other phenomena. The items call for reasoning rather than the recall of information. However, some knowledge of specifics is required of the student.

THE COGNITIVE TAXONOMY—PROBLEMS AND CRITICISMS

Without detracting from the general utility of the system of classifying cognitive behavior developed by Bloom and his associates, a number of questions must be raised concerning (1) the definition of knowledge assumed, (2) the hierarchical order of certain classes of behaviors based upon the premise that the educational process can be viewed as building complex behaviors according to levels of abstraction, (3) the relationship of the taxonomy to problem solving and inquiry–discovery processes, and (4) the relationship of the taxonomy to creative processes.

Knowledge vs. Information

Regarding the definition of knowledge assumed by Bloom and his associates, it can be seen that "knowledge" as represented in the first set of subclasses is little more than the simple recall of information. As discussed earlier, Dewey viewed knowledge as those behaviors that "render our action intelligent," [17] whereas "information severed from thoughtful action . . . is a most powerful obstacle to further growth in the grace of intelligence." [18]

On the other hand, Bloom and his associates have defined knowledge "as little more than the remembering of the idea or phenomenon in a form very close to that in which it was originally encountered," while noting that "probably the most common educational objective in American education is the acquisition of knowledge (sic) or information." [19] Because many educators would not equate "knowledge" with the simple recall of information, the term *knowledge,* as used in the taxonomy, fails to meet an essential criterion of a taxonomy: commonly accepted usage among professionals. Consequently, the term *recall of information* seems to be more appropriate for the taxonomy.

Hierarchical Order

The basic premise upon which the taxonomy was developed is that cognitive learning occurs in a sequential order, from simple to complex behaviors, according to levels of abstractness. However, this premise may be more of a logical ordering of cognitive behaviors rather than a truly valid explanation of the sequential development of various levels of cognitive behavior.

---

[17] Dewey, *Democracy and Education,* op. cit., p. 100.

[18] Ibid., p. 179.

[19] Bloom (ed.), *Taxonomy of Educational Objectives,* op. cit., pp. 28–29.

Criterion of Difficulty. Young children learn to communicate through spoken language long before they enter school. In noting the complex phenomenon by which young children learn to relate the abstract sounds of spoken language to complex life situations, Whitehead challenged the criterion of difficulty by which school studies are arranged and classified.

> I commence by challenging the adequacy of some principles by which the subjects for study are often classified in order. . . . Consider first the criterion of difficulty. It is not true that the easier subjects should precede the harder. On the contrary, some of the hardest must come first because nature so dictates, and because they are essential to life. The first intellectual task which confronts an infant is the acquirement of spoken language. What an appalling task, the correlation of meanings with sounds! It requires an analysis of ideas and an analysis of sounds. We all know that the infant does it, and that the miracle of his achievement is explicable. . . .
>
> What is the next subject in the education of the infant minds? The acquirement of written language; that is to say, the correlation of sounds with shapes. Great heavens! Have our educationists gone mad? . . . I will not elaborate my point further; I merely restate it in the form, that the postponement of difficulty is no safe clue for the maze of educational practice.[20]

To assume that one must first learn the elements of a phenomenon or concept as an antecedent to the understanding and utilization of the material would mean that a child would have to know the alphabet before he could learn to speak. The point is that it is easier to learn many seemingly complex abstractions when such material is understood and utilized in concrete, life-relevant situations than it is to learn the individual elements or components of an abstraction when the components are not applicable to life situations.

Logical vs. Ecological. Thus, the elements or components of a phenomenon may be learned after, not before, the phenomenon is generally understood, made meaningful, and put to use in daily life. Consequently, the hierarchical order of instructional objectives developed by Bloom and his associates may be more of a logical classification system than a psychological and ecological ordering of objectives. By *ecological* we mean the arrangement of phenomena in interaction, according to their effects upon each other. In this sense comprehension is not necessarily a more abstract form of behavior than the rote learning of specific and isolated bits of information. Effective learning requires that comprehension be integral to the task, whether the task is elementary or complex, concrete or abstract.

Moreover, the placement of "application" at a higher level of abstraction than "knowledge" and "comprehension" runs counter to many life situations. As in Whitehead's illustration of language learning, application and comprehension go hand in hand with the learning of language symbols and forms, as well as with other learning tasks.

---

20 Whitehead, op. cit., pp. 25–26.

Relationship to Problem Solving and Inquiry–Discovery Processes

There is considerable disagreement as to the degree of specificity necessary in identifying and evaluating instructional objectives. Bloom notes that when a subject matter is likely to encounter little change in the future, instructional objectives can be developed more systematically and specifically than in the case where the field is open and highly changeable. In the latter case, the focus may be on inquiry objectives and higher mental processes which are used in developing the subject rather than on the subject matter as an end product.[21] In other words, here the emphasis is on utilizing the subject matter as the raw material and as tools for problem-solving and inquiry–discovery processes.

Although Bloom's taxonomy incorporates a number of objectives indigenous to problem-solving and inquiry–discovery processes, it does not focus on these processes per se. Consequently, a student may be engaged in a wide range of cognitive activities in the classroom or laboratory without being consciously aware of the overall processes of problem solving and inquiry–discovery. Ideally, however, the student should be fully aware of the relationship of various cognitive skills to the processes of problem solving and inquiry–discovery.

Relationship to Creative Processes

Although Bloom, Hastings, and Madaus acknowledge that the taxonomy, for the most part, represents convergent thinking, they point out that divergent thinking and creative thinking are possible when the student engages in *synthesis*. Instead of seeking a singularly correct solution, in synthesis the student "may provide a unique response . . . producing ideas, plans, and products which are uniquely his . . . and it is the task of the teacher or evaluator to determine the merits of the responses in terms of the process exhibited, the quality of the product, or the quality of evidence and arguments supporting the synthetic work." [22]

Limitations of Paper-and-Pencil Tests. Although difficult to measure empirically, most teachers are able to find creativity in student stories, poems, essays, arts, crafts, musical compositions, hypothesis formulation in science, and so on. However, because paper-and-pencil tests impose severe time restrictions on the learner, and because the act of creative thinking is not a product of speed, it is doubtful that such tests can serve to stimulate creative thinking to any considerable extent. Even in cases where teachers devise imaginative essay items that deal with provocative problems, the constraint of time makes it unlikely that the student will be able to come up with a creative response.

---

[21] Bloom, "Some Theoretical Issues Relating to Educational Evaluation," in *Educational Evaluation: New Roles, New Means,* op. cit., p. 34.

[22] Benjamin S. Bloom, J. Thomas Hastings, and George F. Madaus, *Handbook on Formative and Summative Evaluation of Student Learning* (New York: McGraw-Hill Book Company, 1971), p. 194.

This does not mean that teachers should abandon their attempts to stimulate creative and divergent thinking through paper-and-pencil tests. Too much of schooling is limited to the inculcation of convergent modes of thought. But in view of the restrictions of paper-and-pencil tests, coupled with the difficulties in predicting and measuring quantitatively the creative act, it would appear that an empirical taxonomy for evaluating creativity as an educational objective has inherent limitations.

Fruitful Mistakes. Perhaps a more fruitful approach would be for teachers to develop classroom, seminar, laboratory, shop, and studio environments designed to stimulate students to think divergently in formulating problems and hypotheses, and in seeking solutions to problems, by engaging in long-term projects. Facilities should be open to students after school. The author has observed high school students absorbed in such projects after school hours, when such activities carry no academic credit. In the conventional classroom or laboratory, with so many lessons and experiments to cover in given time periods and marking periods, the atmosphere can best be described as "nervous," at least for the teacher. Students should have opportunities to make important mistakes and to learn through their mistakes. Tests and conventional teaching seem to be intended to give the student the notion that competent people do not make errors. Yet infallibility is more of a characteristic of the machine; humans are notably fallible.

In everyday life both the gifted man and the common man have opportunities to make errors and to correct their errors. Some of the most important breakthroughs have occurred when gifted men have learned through their mistakes. In traditional schooling the mistake, however trivial, is counted as a penalty and is sometimes treated as if it were a catastrophe. Mistakes can serve an infinitely more useful function in learning than correct answers memorized and reproduced for the examination.

Need for Assessing a Wide Range of Cognitive Objectives

Statements of educational goals frequently call for the development of skills in "critical thinking," "reflective thinking," "problem solving," and, more recently, the skills of "inquiring" and "discovering." Most teachers readily accept such objectives. Yet, although many teachers engage students in a fairly wide variety and range of cognitive styles in day-to-day classroom work, few teachers prepare and make use of devices designed to assess the extent to which they, the teachers, are successful in stimulating students to accomplish these objectives.

As discussed earlier in this book, most teacher-made tests are limited to the lower cognitive levels requiring the mere recall of information and the performance of specific skills in very narrow contexts. Under such circumstances the success of the student is measured by the degree to which he is able and willing to acquire the information and perform the specific operations required by the teacher's tests. Not only is such learning often of little meaning and use to the learner, but it tends to be tedious, boring, and easily forgotten.

When schooling is limited largely to rote tasks and narrowly conceived skills, the learner is denied opportunities to find the patterns and unity which give meaning to the subject matter. Yet it is natural for children and adolescents to seek patterns and unity to make learning meaningful. Unfortunately, when so much school work is limited to the lower cognitive processes, not only does learning acquire a barren quality, but the learner adjusts to this situation by abandoning his normal inclinations to seek real meaning from his studies.

By employing a wide variety and range of cognitive skills in tests and other teaching–learning activities, students will be more likely to gain a richer appreciation of what knowledge is, and will be better able to apply their knowledge to a far broader spectrum of situations in school and in life. Moreover, teachers will be better able to evaluate the effectiveness of the curriculum and to make curriculum decisions that are more likely to produce the desired learning outcomes.

BEHAVIORAL OBJECTIVES

In developing the cognitive taxonomy of educational objectives, Bloom and his associates attempted to identify and classify certain processes of thinking which represent the intended behavior of students as sought by the school. Recognizing the "very real danger" of "fragmentation and atomization of educational purposes," Bloom and his associates endeavored to construct the taxonomy at a reasonable level of generality.[23]

However, the decade of the 1960's witnessed a growing interest in developing detailed specifications for assessing learning outcomes. This interest came about largely as a result of the developments in instructional technology and programmed instruction, and the concern for evaluating the effects of the new federally financed curriculum packages being adopted on an unprecedented scale. The availability of federal funds for curriculum evaluation attracted to the curriculum field many psychologists who sought to evaluate learning outcomes in terms of highly specific, quantifiable "behaviors." Before discussing further the implications of these developments on the contemporary scene, a brief review of some background influences is presented.

The Doctrine of Specification

"Whatever exists at all exists in some amount," wrote Thorndike in 1918.[24] As a leading educational theorist during most of the first half of the twentieth

---

[23] Bloom (ed.), *Taxonomy of Educational Objectives,* op. cit., pp. 5–6.

[24] E. L. Thorndike, in National Society for the Study of Education, *The Measurement of Educational Products,* Seventeenth Yearbook, Part II (Bloomington, Ill.: Public School Publishing Company, 1918), p. 16.

century, Thorndike held that educational objectives must be verified through the measurement of specific practices. He viewed learning as the forming of bonds or connections between specific stimuli and observable responses, a theory which came to be further refined and extended to educational practices by the behaviorists.

Scientific Management. During the early part of the twentieth century, such pioneers in curriculum construction as Franklin Bobbitt and W. W. Charters proceeded to develop ways of reducing educational objectives into measurable component elements. However, in their quest for developing a scientific basis for curriculum construction, these men were influenced more by the scientific management movement in business and industry than by the developing behavioral sciences. For example, Bobbitt called for educators "to set up definite standards for the various educational products" and proceeded to explain that the educational need was for definite specifications and scales of measurement.[25] According to Bobbitt, "the ability to add at a speed of 65 combinations per minute with an accuracy of 94 per cent is as definite a specification as can be set up for any aspect of the work of the steel plant." [26]

The major task in curriculum construction, argued Bobbitt, is to develop specifications based upon a thorough analysis of activities that are necessary for successful adult life. When these activities are determined, the objectives of education become clear. However, the specifications must be measurable. General unanalyzed objectives, such as "ability to care for one's health," are to be avoided because they are too general to be useful. Instead, contended Bobbitt, it must be reduced to particularity, such as "ability to care for the teeth." [27]

The sheer tonnage of such detailed specifications, coupled with the growing influence of the progressive movement and new developments in learning theory, brought about a collapse of activity analysis and other mechanistic approaches to curriculum construction.

Specificity vs. Generality. Nevertheless, the problem of measuring educational achievement and assessing the effectiveness of alternative approaches to curriculum construction remained a continuous concern of educators. Thus, in 1950, Tyler noted that "if we are to study an educational program systematically, we must first be sure as to the educational objectives aimed at." [28] According to Tyler, "the complete definition of the objective includes not only a

[25] Franklin Bobbitt, "Some General Principles of Management Applied to the Problems of City-School Systems," in National Society for the Study of Education, *The Supervision of City Schools,* Twelfth Yearbook, Part I (Bloomington, Ill.: Public School Publishing Company, 1913), p. 11.

[26] Ibid.

[27] Ibid., p. 32.

[28] Ralph W. Tyler, *Basic Principles of Curriculum and Instruction* (Chicago: The University of Chicago Press, 1950), p. 3.

statement of the kind of behavior involved, but also a statement of the kind of content with which the behavior deals." [29]

However, Tyler cautioned against viewing and applying these objectives mechanistically by stressing the need for continuity, sequence, and integration both within subject fields and in relation to the total curriculum.[30] Moreover, his illustrations of behavioral objectives were broadly based, such as "to develop ability to apply principles that are taught in biological science to concrete biological problems that arise in (one's) everyday life." [31] Coupled with a statement of the content aspects of the course of study (such as the subject matter relating to the functions of human organisms, energy relations, and so on), the steps to be taken for the further development of the curriculum can be specified more clearly.[32] But Tyler warned against excessive specificity in defining and measuring behavioral objectives, because educators must not lose sight of "obtaining the level of generality desired and that is in harmony with what we know about the pyschology of learning." [33]

Ironically, it was through the evaluation program of the Eight-Year Study that behavioral objectives emerged as key tools for assessing learning outcomes, despite the fact that these objectives were formulated as broad and generalizable constructs. Many contemporary proponents of behavioral objectives insist on such specificity that the "behavior" is not generalizable; consequently, an operant-conditioning rationale is needed to fill the void.

Cronbach criticizes those who insist that objectives be "defined in terms of behavior" for taking an ultraoperationalist position, because they ignore the larger constructs which cannot be specified and measured in advance, but which apply to future situations (e.g., self-confidence, scientific attitude).[34] Humans are not yet so standardized and mechanical that their behaviors can be shaped, predicted, and assessed in accordance with a catalogue of quantifiable specifications.

Renewed Emphasis on Specification

As mentioned earlier in this book, the federal support of instructional technology, programmed instruction, and new curriculum packages during the 1950's and 1960's created a new interest in the systematization of instruction and in the assessment of learning outcomes.

---

[29] Ibid., p. 42.

[30] Ibid., p. 55.

[31] Ibid., p. 31.

[32] Ibid., pp. 31–35.

[33] Ibid., p. 37.

[34] Lee J. Cronbach, "Validation of Educational Measures," in *Proceedings of the 1969 Invitational Conference on Testing Problems* (Princeton, N.J.: Educational Testing Service, 1970), pp. 49–50.

Operant Conditioning. Many psychologists of the behaviorist school and fellow curriculum workers, as proponents of programmed instruction and the new technology, have insisted on defining behavioral objectives in terms of the highest degree of specificity. "Teaching," declares Skinner, "may be defined as an arrangement of contingencies of reinforcement under which behavior changes," [35] and "the whole process of becoming competent in any field must be divided into a very large number of very small steps, and reinforcement must be contingent upon the accomplishment of each step." [36] Skinner has gained a wide following as a result of the emerging interest in educational technology, despite the severe criticisms leveled at him by some leading scholars. For example, in examining Skinner's theory of operant conditioning (the arrangement of contingencies of reinforcement) as applied to language learning, Chomsky states, "I have been able to find no support whatsoever for the doctrine of Skinner and others." [37] Arthur Koestler, the noted writer, has criticized Skinner on the grounds that the theory of operant conditioning is based upon a "crude slot-machine model" of man, while acknowledging that, more than we realize, we have allowed it to permeate education and our whole culture.[38]

Focus on Lower Cognitive Processes. In recent years many books have appeared on the subject of behavioral objectives and specifications. Although Bloom, Hastings, and Madaus caution that "attempts to specify all the outcomes in advance can have a restrictive influence on both teaching and evaluation," [39] many of the proponents of behavioral objectives insist on such precise specifications that the tendency is to concentrate on the lower cognitive processes while neglecting the higher modes of thought. For example, in contrast to Tyler's more generalizable objectives discussed earlier, Mager offers the following as model types of behavioral objectives:

> Given a list of 35 chemical elements, the learner must be able to recall and write the valences of at least 30.

> The student must be able to correctly solve at least seven simple linear equations within a period of thirty minutes.

> Given a human skeleton, the student must be able to correctly identify by labeling at least 40 of the following bones: (list of bones inserted here).[40]

The ultraspecificity of such "behaviors" would require each teacher and student to work with literally hundreds of thousands of explicit objectives.

---

[35] B. F. Skinner, *The Technology of Teaching* (New York: Appleton-Century-Crofts, Inc., 1968), p. 113.

[36] Ibid., p. 21.

[37] Noam Chomsky, review of *Verbal Behavior* by B. F. Skinner (New York: Appleton-Century-Crofts, Inc., 1957), in *Language*, Vol. 35, 1959, p. 42.

[38] Arthur Koestler, *The Ghost in the Machine* (New York: The Macmillan Company, 1967), p. 4.

[39] Bloom, Hastings, and Madaus, op cit., p. 19.

[40] Robert F. Mager, *Preparing Instructional Objectives* (Palo Alto, Calif.: Fearon Publishers, Inc., 1962), pp. 30, 45, 49.

Although some educators are quick to point out that programmed instruction and technological devices can accomplish this task, other educators view with alarm the atomistic and automatic model of man assumed by the proponents of programmed instruction and the new technology.

Moreover, because behavioral objectives are so explicitly defined, they tend to be limited to the lower cognitive processes of recalling specifics and knowing the ways and means of dealing with specifics. As emphasized throughout Part I of this book, the preoccupation with such lower cognitive tasks has been one of the most severe criticisms leveled at traditional teaching during the twentieth century.

Ironically, such learning is commonly called terminal behavior by its proponents. Yet it was Dewey who warned that information is "dead, a mind-crushing load" when it is separated from thoughtful action.[41] When " 'knowledge,' in the sense of information . . . is treated as an end in itself," observed Dewey, "it not only lets occasions for thinking go unused, but it swamps thinking." [42] "Terminal behavior" may be an appropriate description of such learning because it is so easily, if not deliberately, terminated or forgotten by the learner soon after he has passed the examination. It is not very meaningful simply to commit to memory the valences of X number of chemical elements. Information and skills are the resources of learning—the means of continued learning, and the means of developing knowledge and putting knowledge into action. "If you have much to do with the young as they emerge from school and from the university," observed Whitehead, "you soon note the dulled minds of those whose education has consisted in the acquirement of inert knowledge." [43]

Educational Engineering and Accountability

The efforts to apply scientific management to education during the early part of the twentieth century have been resurrected in the 1970's with the call for "educational engineering," "accountability," and "performance contracting." A former U.S. associate commissioner of education puts it this way:

> . . . American educators now have an opportunity so far-reaching that, with a push from the public, *we can transform our schools within this decade.*
>
> This opportunity springs from several sources: from a new and sophisticated process of management that defines educational goals in measurable terms; from testing programs . . . ; and from the growing acceptance of the idea that the schools, like other sectors of society, are accountable to the public for what they do or fail to do.
>
> These developments make possible a new process to bring to the improvement of education the same ingenuity, craft, and realism that got us to the moon.[44]

---

41 Dewey, *Democracy and Education,* op. cit., p. 179.
42 Ibid., pp. 185–186.
43 Whitehead, op. cit., p. 50.
44 Leon Lessinger, *Every Kid a Winner: Accountability in Education* (Palo Alto, Calif.: Science Research Associates, 1970), p. 3.

He continues:

> . . . what we need is data for all children that shows the educational gain
> produced by specific sequences of teaching.
>
> Once the output of schools is measured in proven learning . . . , the next
> step is to relate learning to its cost. . . . We simply keep accounts of the
> cost of a specific teaching sequence and measure the change in performance
> against a standardized evaluation given before and after it.[45]

This simplistic technological model of education is based in no small measure
on efforts to define instruction and to assay its effectiveness in terms of detailed
and mechanistic behavioral objectives and specifications.

Behavior Modification and Measurement

The national interest in behavioral objectives and specifications generated
during the 1960's led the American Educational Research Association to produce a monograph on the subject based upon a symposium held at a national
meeting of the organization.[46] At the symposium, the chairman of the group
took the position that "the only sensible reason for the educator's engaging in
instruction is to modify the learner's behavior; therefore, these intended
changes must be described in terms of measurable learner behaviors." [47] When
a participant stated the case for more open-ended approaches to instruction,
such as in seminars where the teacher and students engage in discussion, the
chairman argued, "I don't consider this to be instruction." [48] In a later work the
chairman and a co-author made this distinction between instructional and non-
instructional events in the classroom:

> All the teacher has to do is to distinguish between classroom events that are
> the consequence of his instruction and those that transcend his area of mea-
> surable influence. . . . But for those objectives not so describable, the teacher
> should recognize that he is not *teaching,* that the sequence is not *instructional,*
> and that his role has radically switched from instructor of a class of responses
> (sic) to custodian of a wide range of unpredictable outcomes. . . . And if most
> of what the teacher does is not instructional, and therefore not within his
> realm of *responsibility,* he ought to feel more than casually queasy about the
> utility of the time he spends in the classroom.[49]

To limit instruction to measurable specifications not only assumes that all
significant outcomes of instruction are perfectly predictable, but robs the teaching–learning process of the very qualities which make it fresh, original, per-

---

[45] Ibid., p. 9.

[46] W. James Popham et al., *Instructional Objectives* (Chicago: Rand McNally & Company,
1969).

[47] Ibid., p. 35.

[48] Ibid., p. 61.

[49] W. James Popham and Eva L. Baker, *Systematic Instruction* (Englewood Cliffs, N.J.:
Prentice-Hall, Inc., 1970), p. 141.

sonal, and human. And, as discussed later, this mechanistic rationale ignores the value of concomitant or collateral learnings—unanticipated outcomes of instruction that may be longer lasting than the target subject matter itself.

Following Thorndike's dictum that "whatever exists at all exists in some amount," a leading measurement specialist contends that "it is difficult to think of any quality which interests us that cannot also be quantified." [50] However, what is overlooked here is that the very act of quantifying a qualitative concept changes the essential properties of the concept. How does one quantify the aesthetic qualities of a musical composition, a painting, a poem, or a bird in flight? One is not romanticizing human nature in recognizing that the human brain's advantage over the computer lies not in the accuracy with which it stores and retrieves quantified data, but in its ability to handle vague ideas. Norbert Wiener noted that this is one of the chief qualities of the human brain which distinguishes it from the computer because "in poems, in novels, in paintings, the brain seems to find itself able to work very well with material that any computer would have to reject as formless." [51]

Collateral Learning and Humanized Schooling

When instruction is limited only to that subject matter which can be reduced to measurable specifications in advance, educators are imposing a machine model on the human learner and the acts of teaching and learning are robbed of the very personal and original qualities of expression which distinguish man from a machine system. Although educational specifications can help teachers focus more clearly on many kinds of important instructional objectives, and develop more effective techniques of assessing learning outcomes, educators must not lose sight of those qualities of a learning environment which open the way to what Dewey called collateral learning.

> Perhaps the greatest of all pedagogical fallacies is the notion that a person learns only the particular thing he is studying at the time. Collateral learning in the way of formation of enduring attitudes, of likes and dislikes, may be and often is much more important than the spelling lesson or lesson in geography or history that is learned. For these attitudes are fundamentally what count in the future. . . . What avail is it to win prescribed amounts of information about geography and history . . . if in the process the individual loses his own soul: loses his appreciation of things worth while, of the values to which these things are relative; if he loses desire to apply what he has learned and, above all, loses the ability to extract meaning from his future experiences as they occur? [52]

In the face of efforts to develop a new technology of teaching, there are strong counterforces calling for a more humanized school. "Our most pressing

---

[50] Robert L. Ebel, *Measuring Educational Achievement* (Englewood Cliffs, N.J.: Prentice-Hall, Inc., 1965), p. 26.

[51] Norbert Wiener, *God and Golem, Inc.* (Cambridge, Mass.: The M.I.T. Press, 1964), p. 73.

[52] Dewey, *Experience and Education*, op. cit., pp. 48–49.

educational problem," notes a contemporary critic, "is not how to increase the efficiency of the schools; it is how to create and maintain a humane society. A society whose schools are inhumane is not likely to be humane itself." [53]

In the final analysis, the test of the value of an education is not in the degree to which the learner is controlled by schooling, but in the ways in which the learner controls his own destiny in society.

SUMMARY

In traditional schooling a student's success is measured to a great extent by his ability to recall specific information and his skill in the ways and means of dealing with specifics in the narrowest of contexts. Because so much of this kind of "learning" is devoid of real comprehension and because there is relatively little opportunity for practical application and meaningful analysis, synthesis, and evaluation, the student tends to forget rather quickly most of what he is tested for on teacher-made examinations. The material to be learned is useful to the student only in the sense that it enables him to obtain the necessary grade. Otherwise, his demonstrated "knowledge" is inert or, even worse, detracts him from engaging in thought-provoking activity. Education should be a process whereby the student learns to utilize knowledge as thought, and the test is one of the tools toward this end.

When the material to be learned is limited largely to the lower cognitive levels, it tends to be mechanical, repetitive, and boring, with the result that students develop poor attitudes toward learning and schooling. Moreover, cognitive learning at any level is not independent of the attitudes, interests, appreciations, and values of the learner. Thus, the high-achieving student in mathematics, for example, may have cultivated a dislike for mathematics as a result of the way he was required to learn mathematics.

Knowledge does not exist apart from the emotions except in the computer. Whereas the computer is far more efficient than man in storing and retrieving information and in interpolating quantitative data, it is man who creates the questions to be solved by the computer and it is man who decides what is to be done with the answers to these questions. Moreover, whereas the computer cannot handle vague ideas, such as social issues involving values and appreciations, humans encounter little difficulty with these ideas. Yet many teachers persist in limiting students to tests that assess pupil achievement primarily in terms of cognitive "knowledge" that is far better suited to the computer.

Too much emphasis is given to the use of teacher-made tests for purposes of assigning grades, rather than for assaying student growth and competence in applying what is learned in a wide variety of life-related situations. Furthermore, teachers need to employ tests in relation to other evaluative techniques and procedures for purposes of assessing the effectiveness of the instructional

---

[53] Charles E. Silberman, *Crisis in the Classroom* (New York: Random House, Inc., 1970), p. 203.

program. Through on-going evaluation during the entire course or instructional program (formative evaluation), teachers and students can benefit from the diagnoses provided by continuous feedback. Teaching–learning strategies can be altered as a result of the diagnoses that are possible through formative evaluation. The summative evaluation, or the evaluation conducted at the end of the course or instructional program, similarly should not be limited to the assignment of grades. Summative evaluation can serve an invaluable function in assessing the success of the course and in comparing the results of different curriculum approaches.

In recent years increasing attention has been given to behavioral objectives and specifications as a result of developments in programmed learning and instructional technology, along with the concern for evaluating the outcomes of the new curriculum packages. Although behavioral objectives were originally conceived to provide a needed linkage between curriculum content and desired behaviors, many proponents of such objectives have become so obsessed with detailed specifications that the learning outcomes being measured represent atomistic bits and pieces of "knowledge" rather than generalized behaviors. As a consequence, such detailed specifications often have a restrictive influence on teaching and learning, because the teacher and learner are required to function in a closed rather than an open system. Learning loses its artistic and adventurous possibilities when virtually every bit of learned behavior must be specified in advance. Moreover, because the lower cognitive skills are most amenable to specificity, such skills tend to receive disproportionate emphasis when "knowledge" is reduced to specifications for programmed instruction.

Not since the early years of the twentieth century has the concern for improving educational efficiency and developing methods of accountability received so much attention. The progressive era of the 1930's and 1940's countered the influences for managerial efficiency in education. The new instructional technology of the 1970's is being countered by a resurgent call for a more humanized school.

PROBLEMS FOR STUDY AND DISCUSSION

1. Examine some teacher-made tests and evaluate each item according to the cognitive levels represented in Bloom's *Taxonomy of Educational Objectives*. What cognitive levels receive the greatest emphasis? What cognitive levels are totally neglected? Can you devise some test items that represent the cognitive levels of *application, analysis, synthesis,* and *evaluation?*

2. What limitations do you see in the uses of taxonomies for identifying and assessing learning outcomes?

3. Norbert Wiener noted that the human brain is able to handle value ideas —ideas that are not quantifiable and that any computer would have to reject as formless. [Norbert Wiener, *God and Golem, Inc.* (Cambridge, Mass.:

The M.I.T. Press, 1964), p. 73.] Yet some proponents of behavioral objectives contend that the teacher is not engaged in *instruction* when dealing with objectives that are not describable in terms that can be quantifiably measured. [W. James Popham and Eva L. Baker, *Systematic Instruction* (Englewood Cliffs, N.J.: Prentice-Hall, Inc., 1970), p. 141.] What are your views on this issue of measuring learning outcomes in connection with educational objectives?

4. In the literature on learning is there general agreement on "laws" which reveal that "all behavior is controlled," as contended in the following statement?

> All behavior is inevitably controlled, and the operation of psychological laws cannot be suspended by romantic conceptions of human behavior, any more than indignant rejection of the law of gravity as antihumanistic can stop people from falling. [Albert Bandura, *Principles of Behavior Modification* (New York: Holt, Rinehart and Winston, Inc., 1969), p. 85.]

How does one identify and explain the "controls" which result in a creative production, such as a symphony by Brahms, a theory by Einstein, or a painting by Cézanne?

5. Dewey observed that "to talk about an educational aim when approximately each act of a pupil is dictated by the teacher, when the only order in the sequence of his acts is that which comes from the assignment of lessons and the giving of directions by another, is sheer nonsense." [John Dewey, *Democracy and Education* (New York: The Macmillan Company, 1916), pp. 118–119.] What implications does this view have for behavioral specifications and programmed instruction? Do you agree with Dewey? Explain.

6. In life the worth of a scientist, an engineer, a baker, or a plumber is not judged by scores on paper-and-pencil tests. Why do such tests occupy a position of such central importance in our schools? What functions should teacher-made tests serve other than grading pupils? Can you envision a school without examinations? Explain.

7. Interview some teachers of different subjects and find out the extent to which pupil grades are determined according to (a) test results and (b) other performance criteria. On the basis of your findings, do you believe that too much emphasis is being given to tests for purposes of grading students?

8. Citing the emerging testing programs and the "new and sophisticated process of management that defines educational goals in *measurable* terms," a former U.S. associate commissioner of education urges educators to adopt a system of educational engineering—"a method of management that uses engineering insights on which leading firms rely—but which our schools have largely ignored." [Leon M. Lessinger, *Every Kid a Winner: Account-*

ability in Education (Palo Alto, Calif.: Science Research Associates, 1970), p. 3.] Do you believe that it is possible and desirable to apply the engineering and management techniques of business and industry to education? Explain.

9. "Knowledge does not keep any better than fish," observed Whitehead. [Alfred North Whitehead, *The Aims of Education and Other Essays* (New York: The Macmillan Company, 1929), p. 147.] What would your opinion be of a dentist or physician who had to rely on his college lecture notes? What implications does Whitehead's view have for the curriculum and the evaluation of learning outcomes in the secondary school?

SELECTED REFERENCES

Aylesworth, Thomas G., and Gerald M. Reagan. *Teaching for Thinking.* Garden City, N.Y.: Doubleday & Company, Inc., 1969.

Bandura, Albert. *Principles of Behavior Modification.* New York: Holt, Rinehart and Winston, Inc., 1969.

Bloom, Benjamin S. (ed.). *Taxonomy of Educational Objectives, Handbook I: Cognitive Domain.* New York: David McKay Company, Inc., 1956.

Bloom, Benjamin S., J. Thomas Hastings, and George F. Madaus. *Handbook on Formative and Summative Evaluation of Student Learning.* New York: McGraw-Hill Book Company, 1971.

Bruner, Jerome S. *The Process of Education.* Cambridge, Mass.: Harvard University Press, 1960.

Callahan, Raymond E. *Education and the Cult of Efficiency.* Chicago: The University of Chicago Press, 1962.

Dewey, John. *Democracy and Education.* New York: The Macmillan Company, 1916.

————. *How We Think.* Lexington, Mass.: D. C. Heath and Company, 1933.

————. *Experience and Education.* New York: The Macmillan Company, 1938.

Dressel, Paul L., et al. *Evaluation in Higher Education.* Boston: Houghton Mifflin Company, 1961.

Dressel, Paul L., and Lewis B. Mayhew. *General Education—Explorations in Evaluation.* Washington, D.C.: American Council on Education, 1954.

Ebel, Robert L. *Measuring Educational Achievement.* Englewood Cliffs, N.J.: Prentice-Hall, Inc., 1965.

Eisner, Elliot W. (ed.). *Confronting Curriculum Reform.* Boston: Little, Brown and Company, 1971.

French, Will, et al. *Behavioral Goals of General Education in High School.* New York: Russell Sage Foundation, 1957.

Grobman, Hulda. *Developmental Curriculum Projects: Decision Points and Processes.* Itasca, Ill.: F. E. Peacock, Publishers, Inc., 1970. Ch. 3.

Gronlund, Norman E. *Stating Behavioral Objectives for Classroom Instruction.* New York: The Macmillan Company, 1970.

Hullfish, H. Gordon, and Philip G. Smith. *Reflective Thinking: The Method of Education.* New York: Dodd, Mead & Company, 1961.

Koestler, Arthur. *The Ghost in the Machine.* New York: The Macmillan Company, 1967.

Krathwohl, David R., Benjamin S. Bloom, and Bertram B. Masia. *Taxonomy of Educational Objectives, Handbook II: Affective Domain.* New York: David McKay Company, Inc., 1964.

Lessinger, Leon. *Every Kid a Winner: Accountability in Education.* Palo Alto, Calif.: Science Research Associates, 1970.

Mager, Robert F. *Preparing Instructional Objectives.* Palo Alto, Calif.: Fearon Publishers, Inc., 1962.

National Society for the Study of Education. *Educational Evaluation: New Roles, New Means.* Sixty-eighth Yearbook, Part II. Chicago: The University of Chicago Press, 1969.

Piaget, Jean. *The Psychology of Intelligence* (1947), translated by M. Piercy and D. E. Berlyne. Paterson, N.J.: Littlefield, Adams, & Company, 1960.

Popham, W. James, et al. *Instructional Objectives.* Chicago: Rand McNally & Company, 1969.

Scriven, Michael. *The Methodology of Evaluation.* Chicago: Rand McNally & Company, 1967.

Shulman, Lee S., and Evan R. Kieslar (eds.). *Learning by Discovery: A Critical Appraisal.* Chicago: Rand McNally & Company, 1966.

Silberman, Charles E. *Crisis in the Classroom.* New York: Random House, Inc., 1970.

Skinner, B. F. *The Technology of Teaching.* New York: Appleton-Century-Crofts, Inc., 1968.

———. *Beyond Freedom and Dignity.* New York: Alfred A. Knopf, Inc., 1971.

Taba, Hilda. *Curriculum Development—Theory and Practice.* New York: Harcourt Brace Jovanovich, Inc., 1962. Chs. 12, 18, 19.

Tanner, Daniel. *Secondary Curriculum—Theory and Development.* New York: The Macmillan Company, 1971. Chs. 1, 2, 11.

Tyler, Ralph W. *Basic Principles of Curriculum and Instruction.* Chicago: The University of Chicago Press, 1950.

Wiener, Norbert. *God and Golem, Inc.* Cambridge, Mass.: The M.I.T. Press, 1964.

Whitehead, Alfred North. *The Aims of Education and Other Essays.* New York: The Macmillan Company, 1929.

Part II

Instructional Goals and Outcomes
—Affective Objectives

"A gifted man cannot handle bacteria or equations without taking fire from what he does and having his emotions engaged," observed a scientist.[1] The common man, like the gifted man, does not deal with knowledge in the absence of feelings or emotions. How many students have cultivated a dislike for mathematics or Shakespeare because of the way in which they were made to encounter these subject matters in the classroom?

Almost everyone can recall some classroom learning experience which resulted in either a strongly negative or positive attitude toward a given subject matter. Although some students are able to perform satisfactorily even when their attitude toward the particular subject is not favorable, in general, attitudes are closely related to achievement.

As discussed in Part I, cognitive and affective factors are virtually interdependent in the teaching–learning process. However, in view of the tendency to ignore or neglect the evaluation of affective outcomes, special attention is devoted to affective learning in this section.

THE NECESSARY INTERDEPENDENCE OF AFFECTIVE AND COGNITIVE PROCESSES

In Part I of this book, the importance of focusing on a wide range of cognitive processes was stressed on the grounds that knowledge is not merely a store of information and, thus, cannot be measured in terms of one's ability to recall or regurgitate mere information. Knowledge is both the resource and product of thought. And if education is to be thought-provoking, knowl-

---

[1] J. Bronowski, "The Creative Process," in *Science and Society*, Thomas D. Clareson (ed.) (New York: Harper & Row, Publishers, 1961), p. 47.

edge cannot exist apart from the understandings which "enable us to adapt our aims and desires to the situation in which we live." [2]

In this sense education involves not only the processes of comprehension, analysis, and synthesis of subject matter, but the evaluation and application of the material in the context of new situations and problems. And the application of knowledge or of an idea, according to Whitehead, means "relating it to that stream, compounded of sense perceptions, feelings, hopes, desires, and of mental activities adjusting thought to thought, which forms our life." [3] To summarize Dewey, intellectual force does not exist apart from the attitudes, feelings, or emotions which make us open-minded rather than closed-minded, responsible rather than irresponsible.[4]

Despite the general recognition that cognitive processes are inseparable from affective processes, Bloom and others note that "American education has failed to emphasize affective goals," and that "teacher-made tests used to assess student performance are geared almost exclusively to cognitive outcomes." [5] As a consequence, noted Whitehead, "the craving for expansion, for activity, inherent in youth is disgusted by a dry imposition of disciplined knowledge." [6]

Achievement, Affective Influences, and Curriculum Reform Projects

Instruments and procedures for assessing the relationship of affective influences on achievement leave much to be desired. Nevertheless, most educators assume that high achievement is associated with high interest, and a number of studies have shown this generally to be the case.[7] For example, a large-scale international study of achievement in mathematics found that interest in mathematics is positively related to achievement, although it was also found that a relatively large number of high-achieving students indicated that they had no desire or intention of taking further work in mathematics.[8]

Although these findings on first inspection appear to be paradoxical, the researchers concluded that the lack of desire on the part of high-achieving students in mathematics to continue their studies in this subject may have been "a result of a pressure toward high achievement in mathematics." [9] In other

---

[2] John Dewey, *Democracy and Education* (New York: The Macmillan Company, 1916), p. 400.

[3] Alfred North Whitehead, *The Aims of Education* (New York: The Macmillan Company, 1929), p. 4.

[4] See John Dewey, *How We Think* (Lexington, Mass.: D. C. Heath and Company, 1933), pp. 28–33.

[5] Benjamin S. Bloom, J. Thomas Hastings, and George F. Madaus, *Handbook on Formative and Summative Evaluation of Student Learning* (New York: McGraw-Hill Book Company, 1971), p. 226.

[6] Whitehead, op. cit., p. 50.

[7] Torsten Husén (ed.), *International Study of Achievement in Mathematics,* Vol. II (New York: John Wiley & Sons, 1967), p. 146.

[8] Ibid., pp. 153, 157.

[9] Ibid., p. 157.

words, external pressures may spur students toward high achievement, but such pressures may also result in negative attitudes toward pursuing the subject matter. This finding has profound implications for career goals.

Unanticipated Outcomes

Educators should not assume that pressuring students toward high achievement will produce a commitment on the part of these students toward further study in the particular subject. Affective influences cannot be ignored in the drive for academic excellence.

A notable example was the national effort during the 1950's and 1960's to increase the proportion of students enrolled in high school and college physics, and to increase the number of students electing careers in this field. The new high school physics produced in 1960 by the Physical Science Study Committee (PSSC), through the expenditure of millions of dollars in grants from the National Science Foundation, was designed to bring about marked increases in enrollments and in the "supply" of physicists.

Instead, however, these efforts were followed by a significant decline in the proportion of high school students enrolled in physics, as well as a decline in the proportion of college students majoring in physics during the ten-year period following Sputnik I. This decline has been attributed, in part at least, to the tendency of the curriculum reformers to ignore adolescent interests.[10] The curriculum reformers, most of whom were university physicists, developed the new high school physics to reflect their own interests in their discipline while neglecting the interests of adolescents.

Emergence of Alternative Approaches

As a consequence of the unanticipated results of their efforts, new physics courses were introduced in 1969 and 1970 which included topics emphasizing the applications of physics in belated recognition that most adolescents are interested in the practical applications of subject matter. Similar changes in emphasis have emerged in other fields, particularly in the social studies, where the demand for life relevance has called for problem-centered and issue-centered approaches.

Thus, the discipline-centered curriculum projects of the 1950's and 1960's are being modified, and alternative approaches to curriculum construction are emerging in recognition that adolescent interests are not identical to those of the mature scholar-researcher who is at the forefront of his specialized discipline. Some implications of these developments are discussed later with particular reference to affective considerations.

---

[10] See *Carnegie Quarterly*, Vol. 18 (Fall, 1970), pp. 5–6; and Donivan J. Watley and Robert C. Nichols, *Career Decisions of Talented Youth: Trends Over the Past Decade* (Evanston, Ill.: National Merit Scholarship Corporation, 1969).

CLASSIFICATION OF AFFECTIVE OBJECTIVES

The development of the taxonomy of cognitive objectives led Krathwohl, Bloom, and Masia to construct an affective taxonomy, also along the lines of a hierarchical continuum.[11] The following is a succinct description of the affective continuum:

> At the lowest point on this continuum, the subject is merely aware of a phenomenon, simply able to perceive it. At the next level he is willing to attend to the phenomenon. The next step finds him responding to the phenomenon with feeling. At the next point the subject goes out of his way to respond to the phenomenon. Next he conceptualizes his behavior and feelings and organizes these into a structure. The subject reaches the highest point in the hierarchy when the structure becomes (part of) his life outlook.[12]

Obviously, the processes just described are closely intertwined with cognitive learning. The developers of the affective taxonomy are careful to stress that their "split between the affective and cognitive domains is for analytical purposes and is quite arbitrary." [13] A highly condensed version of the affective taxonomy is presented as follows: [14]

Affective Taxonomy

1.0 Receiving (Attending)
Sensitivity to the existence of a given condition, phenomenon, situation, or problem.

    1.1 *Awareness*
Conscious recognition of the actual existence of a given condition, phenomenon, situation, or problem (e.g., awareness of aesthetic factors in architecture).

    1.2 *Willingness to Receive*
Willingness to tolerate or take notice of a given phenomenon (etc.) rather than to avoid it (e.g., listens attentively to what others have to say).

    1.3 *Controlled or Selected Attention*
Differentiation, selection, or discrimination among various aspects of a phenomenon (etc.), or control of attention toward aspects of the phenomenon (e.g., listens to music with some discrimination as to mood and effect).

2.0 Responding
Reaction to a phenomenon (etc.) through overt response, or doing something with, or as a result of, a given phenomenon.

    2.1 *Acquiescence in Responding*
Compliance with a given condition (e.g., obeys traffic regulations).

---

11 David R. Krathwohl, Benjamin S. Bloom, and Bertram B. Masia, *Taxonomy of Educational Objectives, Handbook II: Affective Domain* (New York: David McKay Company, Inc., 1964), pp. 176–185.

12 Bloom, Hastings, and Madaus, op. cit., p. 229.

13 Krathwohl, Bloom, and Masia, op. cit., p. 62.

14 Adapted from Krathwohl, Bloom, and Masia, ibid., pp. 176–185.

2.2 *Willingness to Respond*

Voluntary action ("on one's own") in relation to a given phenomenon (e.g., voluntarily reads the daily newspaper and discusses current affairs).

2.3 *Satisfaction in Response*

Enjoyment in acting on a given phenomenon (e.g., enjoys playing the piano or reading literature).

3.0 Valuing

Attachment of worth or belief in a phenomenon (etc.) with some degree of consistency.

3.1 *Acceptance of a Value*

Belief in a proposition, condition, doctrine (etc.) with reasonable but tentative certainty (e.g., agrees that women should receive equal pay for equal work).

3.2 *Preference for a Value*

Belief in the desirability or necessity of a proposition, condition (etc.) over corresponding alternatives (e.g., deliberately seeks the views of others on controversial issues with a view toward forming one's own opinions).

3.3 *Commitment to a Value*

Conviction and full involvement in a cause, principle, or doctrine (e.g., writes letter to editor protesting censorship in any form).

4.0 Organization

Development of values as an organized system, including the determination of their interrelationships, and the establishment of value priorities.

4.1 *Conceptualization of a Value*

Comprehension of the relationship of abstract elements of a value to those already held or to new values that are gaining one's acceptance (e.g., identifies the characteristics of classical music, which he admires and enjoys, in relation to rock and roll, which he dislikes).

4.2 *Organization of a Value System*

Development of a complex of values, including disparate values, in terms of an ordered relationship which, ideally, is harmonious and internally consistent (e.g., weighs alternative social policies and practices in terms of the need to promote the public welfare rather than the aggrandizement of special interests).

5.0 Characterization by a Value or Value Complex

Synthesis and internalization of a value system that is organized in a sufficiently harmonious and pervasive way so as to lead the individual to act consistently in accordance with the values, beliefs, or ideals which comprise his total philosophy or world view.

5.1 *Generalized Set*

Orientation enabling the individual to reduce and order the complex environment and to act consistently and effectively in it (e.g., readiness to revise judgments and to change behavior in the light of valid evidence).

5.2 *Characterization*

Internalization of a value system having as its objective the whole of what is known and knowable in a consistent and harmonious relationship (e.g., regulates one's personal and civic life according to a code of behavior based on ethical principles consistent with democratic ideals).

THE AFFECTIVE TAXONOMY—ILLUSTRATIVE TEST ITEMS

Before discussing the pervading problems and criticisms connected with attempts at evaluating affective outcomes of the teaching–learning process, some items are presented in this section to illustrate how the affective taxonomy may be applied in the construction of tests. Although the question as to whether students should be assigned grades in accordance with their affective learning outcomes is discussed in some detail later in this book, some discussion of this question is appropriate before presenting the sample test items.

Affective Achievement and the Issue of Grading

In reviewing the affective taxonomy, it can be seen that merely by virtue of taking any ordinary test on cognitive achievement, the student is engaged in the act of *receiving* (exhibiting *awareness,* willingness *to receive,* and *controlled or selected attention*), along with the act of *responding* (exhibiting either *acquiescence* or *willingness to respond*). However, the real issue in grading students on affective achievement does not apply to these lower levels of the affective taxonomy, but rather to the higher levels of *satisfaction in response* (attitudes, for example) and *valuing.* Consequently, our discussion in this section of the issue of whether students are to be graded according to their affective achievement is directed at the higher affective levels of the taxonomy.

Before discussing this issue further it is important to differentiate between tests that are designed primarily to evaluate affective outcomes and those that deal with affective learning as integrally related to cognitive learning. In the former case, the purpose is not to grade the student, but to provide evaluative feedback for the teacher and curriculum worker concerning the effectiveness of the course or unit of study. In this connection feedback may also be provided for the student, so that he can gain a better understanding of his own attitudes, interests, values, and so on. But again no constructive purpose is served by grading students on so-called purely affective outcomes. Such grading would only force the student to seek the "right" answer, rather than to interpret the items in terms of his actual attitudes, interests, values, or even biases.

On the other hand, when tests are designed to evaluate cognitive outcomes in connection with affective learning, it is possible to grade students according to their achievement levels; however, such grading would be directed at assessing cognitive outcomes rather than affective outcomes. For example, students might be asked to indicate their position on a controversial issue, and then to justify their position with all the pertinent evidence at their disposal. The responses would then be graded not according to which side of the issue a student takes, but according to his ability to evaluate the issue in the light of all pertinent evidence. A similar procedure could be employed in evaluating and supporting one's preferences for works in art, music, or literature—or in evaluating conflicting evidence on a controversial question in science. Although the grading of such tests is directed at cognitive outcomes, the teacher and students are gaining invaluable feedback on affective learning outcomes. Moreover, such tests can be used as important instructional tools.

As emphasized in Part I, however, paper-and-pencil tests can measure only a fraction of the actual cognitive learning that occurs in school. Regarding affective learning outcomes, paper-and-pencil tests present even more severe limitations, not only because the evaluation of affective objectives has been so neglected over the years, but because such objectives are difficult to identify and measure with a high degree of validity. Nevertheless, coupled with the assessment of student motivations, interests, and attitudes as evidenced in student performance in a variety of learning activities—such as projects, themes, panel discussions, class discussions, written and oral reports, library work, laboratory work, and so on—tests designed to measure affective outcomes can make a most valuable contribution toward the improvement of classroom teaching and learning.

Evaluating Affective Outcomes—Sample Items

No attempt is made in this section to present a comprehensive overview of test construction. Instead, emphasis is given to developing some understanding of the ways through which teacher-made tests can be used to evaluate important affective outcomes in relation to cognitive learning. "As educators," notes one writer, "we have devoted almost exclusive attention to intellectual and cognitive processes . . . (because) we do not understand the relationship between feelings and intellectual behavior." [15] In this connection, some illustrative test items are presented to stimulate the reader to think about some ways through which teachers may focus their attention on an area that has been long neglected.

The following items are adapted from an instrument developed for the Eight-Year Study for purposes of evaluating students' interests in voluntary reading:

> *Directions:* Consider each question carefully and answer it as *honestly* and as *frankly* as you possibly can. There are three ways to mark your answer in the blank space before each item:
>
> *Y* means that your answer is *Yes.*
> *U* means that your answer is *Uncertain.*
> *N* means that your answer is *No.*

---

15 Walcott H. Beatty (ed.), *Improving Educational Assessment and an Inventory of Measures of Affective Behavior* (Washington, D.C.: Association for Supervision and Curriculum Development, NEA, 1969), pp. 74–75.

_____1. Do you have in mind one or two books which you would like to read sometime soon?

_____2. Are there any well-known works of English or American literature which you would like to read during your leisure time?

_____3. Do you ever read essays, apart from school requirements?

_____4. Have you ever done further reading in an attempt to learn more about the period, the event, or the places presented in a book which you have read?

_____5. Do you read the book-review sections of magazines or newspapers fairly regularly?

_____6. Do you often discuss with friends such questions as what the most popular current books are, what makes a book a best seller, and the like?

_____7. Is it very unusual for you, of your own accord, to look up information about the life of an author after reading one of his books? [16]

In their taxonomy Krathwohl, Bloom, and Masia classify the preceding items 1 and 2 as *willingness to receive,* items 3 and 4 as *acquiescence in responding,* and items 5, 6, and 7 as *willingness to respond.*[17] Obviously, the preceding items were designed not to be used in grading students on their affective achievement, but rather to assay differences in the affective responses of student populations exposed to different educational conditions or treatments. Such items also could be useful to teachers who are interested in assessing affective outcomes. However, as constructed, the preceding items may suffer from the tendency of many students to respond in accordance with their perceptions of the desired expectations of the project director or teacher. In other words, the items can be manipulated easily by the students, thereby giving the project director or teacher invalid data. As a means of improving the validity of the answers, the items might be redesigned as follows:

Directions: Consider each question carefully and answer it as *honestly* and as *frankly* as you possibly can. In the blank space before each item mark your answer in one of three ways:

 Y means that your answer is *Yes.*
 U means that your answer is *Uncertain.*
 N means that your answer is *No.*

Whenever your answer to an item is either *Y* (*Yes*) or *U* (*Uncertain*), fill in the blank spaces following the item.

_____1. Do you have in mind one or two books which you would like to read sometime soon?

Title	Author
a. _____	_____
b. _____	_____

---

[16] Adapted from *Questionnaire on Voluntary Reading* (Chicago: Evaluation in the Eight-Year Study, Progressive Education Association, 1940).

[17] Krathwohl, Bloom, and Masia, op. cit., pp. 124–129.

_____2. Are there any well-known works of English or American literature which you would like to read during your leisure time?

                                      Title   Author

a. _____   _____

b. _____   _____

Evaluating Affective Outcomes in Relation to Cognitive Outcomes—Sample Items

Validation of the responses relating to affective outcomes is sought in the preceding illustrations by requiring the student to provide supporting evidence from the cognitive domain (*knowledge or specifics or recall of specific information*).

In evaluating the affective impact of a unit or course, the teacher or project evaluator also will want to ascertain the extent to which the students take *satisfaction in response*. The following exercise in mathematics illustrates how affective outcomes (*satisfaction in response*) can be assessed along with cognitive outcomes (*knowledge of specifics, translation,* and *application*), although the students would be graded on the latter only:

1. $(1.3 \times 10^5)(1.2 \times 10^3) = $ _____.
2. The period of the moon's revolution around the earth is expressed as 2.36×10^6 seconds. How many *days* does it take the moon to make *one* revolution around the earth? _____ days. (Carry your answer to the nearest tenth.)
3. Of the two preceding problems, I like the second problem
   _____a. a lot more.
   _____b. a little more.
   _____c. a little less.
   _____d. a lot less.
   _____e. about the same.
4. What is your chief reason for your answer to question 3? _____

     _____

     _____

Another set of items (mathematics and social studies) also is designed to assess certain cognitive outcomes (e.g., *knowledge of ways and means of dealing with specifics, translation, interpretation, application,* and *analysis*), along with affective outcomes (*satisfaction in response*):

1. a. Express 1.73 as a per cent of 0.69 _____.
   b. Express 2.3 as a per cent of 0.498 _____.
2. In 1966 New York City spent $0.86 billion for education, as compared with $1.50 billion for education in 1971. During the same period, the City's expenditures for welfare increased from $0.494 billion to $2.1 billion.
   a. By what per cent did the expenditures for education increase between 1966 and 1971? _____%.

b. By what per cent did the expenditures for welfare increase between 1966 and 1971? _____%.

Some Major Expenditures, New York City Budget, 1966 and 1971

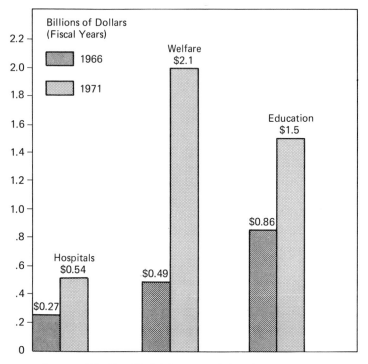

Source: The New York Times, March 7, 1971, p. 1E.

Directions: Answer problem 3 with reference to the data in the above graph.

3. a. By what per cent did the expenditures for hospitals increase between 1966 and 1971? _____%.

    b. By what per cent did the expenditures increase for education and welfare combined during this period? _____%.

4. In comparing problems 1a and 1b with problems 2a and 2b, I like problems 1a and 1b

    _____a. a lot more.

    _____b. a little more.

    _____c. a little less.

    _____d. a lot less.

    _____e. about the same.

5. What is your chief reason for your answer to question 4? _____
    _____
    _____

6. In comparing problems 2a and 2b with problems 3a and 3b, I like problems 2a and 2b
    _____a. a lot more.
    _____b. a little more.
    _____c. a little less.
    _____d. a lot less.
    _____e. about the same.
7. What is your chief reason for your answer to question 6? _____

_____

8. In comparing problems 1a and 1b with problems 3a and 3b, I like problems 1a and 1b
    _____a. a lot more.
    _____b. a little more.
    _____c. a little less.
    _____d. a lot less.
    _____e. about the same.
9. What is your chief reason for your answer to question 8? _____

_____

10. The comments below were made by the news writer in the article in which the preceding graph appeared. Interpret each comment by placing the appropriate symbol in each blank.

    F—a fact derived from data in the graph
    FN—a fact not derived from data in the graph
    O—an opinion supported by data in the graph
    ON—an opinion not supported by data in the graph

    __FN__   a. "One out of seven New Yorkers is already on relief
    __FN__   b. "and the welfare bill is more than the total 1959 city budget.
    __F__   c. "Welfare is a bigger item than education in the city budget
    __ON__   d. "and it's also a national scandal—
    __FN__   e. "the federal government only pays a third of the cost, with the state and city splitting the rest."

11. Write a meaningful paragraph using the following terms:
    welfare
    poverty
    federal government
    migration
    urbanization
    unemployment

Regarding item 11, the teacher may want to encourage students to express their attitudes and values on the related concepts. In so doing, the teacher should stress that the students are free to express their opinions and that their answers will be evaluated not on their opinions but on their ability to relate these concepts in a meaningful way. Answers reflecting sharply conflicting attitudes and values on the part of different students can be used for follow-up class discussions, library assignments, panel reports, and other learning activities to enable students to explore different sides of value-laden problems or issues.

Yet another set of items illustrates how cognitive skills (e.g., *interpretation, extrapolation, application,* and *analysis*) can be assessed in conjunction with affective learning (*attitudes* and *values*): [18]

Read the following quotation from Alexander Hamilton in *The Federalist,* October 27, 1787:

So numerous indeed and so powerful are the causes which serve to give a false bias to the judgment, that we, upon many occasions, see wise and good men on the wrong as well as on the right side of questions of the first magnitude to society. This circumstance, if duly attended to, would furnish a lesson of moderation to those who are ever so much persuaded of their being in the right in any controversy. And a further reason for caution, in this respect, might be drawn from the reflection that we are not always sure that those who advocate the truth are influenced by purer principles than their antagonists. Ambition, avarice, personal animosity, party opposition and many other motives not more laudable than these, are apt to operate as well upon those who support as those who oppose the right side of a question. . . . In politics as in religion, it is equally absurd to aim at making proselytes by fire and sword. Heresies in either can rarely be cured by persecution.

1. From the information provided by the preceding quotation, mark each of the following statements

    A—If it can be inferred that Hamilton would have *agreed* with the statement.
    D—If it can be inferred that Hamilton would have *disagreed* with the statement.
    N—If no inference can be drawn about Hamilton's probable opinion.

    __D__ a. Compulsory loyalty oaths are the best protection against subversive activities.
    __D__ b. A man's political affiliations are a reliable proof of his principles.
    __A__ c. Political groups are apt to include men of widely differing motives and philosophies.
    __N__ d. Government should be based upon the principle of separation of powers.

2. Indicate your own opinion on each of the following statements by marking the following blanks.

    A—If you *agree* with the statement.
    D—If you *disagree* with the statement.

---

[18] Adapted from Paul L. Dressel et al., *Evaluation in Higher Education* (Boston: Houghton Mifflin Company, 1961), pp. 99–100.

_____a. Compulsory loyalty oaths are the best protection against subversive activities.

_____b. A man's political affiliations are a reliable proof of his principles.

_____c. Political groups are apt to include men of widely differing motives and philosophies.

_____d. Government should be based upon the principle of separation of powers.

3. In two short essays, support your opinion on the preceding statements *a* and *c* by discussing their relevance to contemporary affairs in the light of recent history.

The preceding essay item allows the student to express his *acceptance, preference,* or *commitment* on certain sociopolitical values, and to express his *conceptualization* of certain *values,* while possibly relating these to his own *value system.* At the same time he is required to support his answers with relevant data from contemporary and historic events. Obviously, the student is not graded on his opinions or values, but according to his ability to support his position with relevant data.

A series of items in the fine arts illustrates how cognitive skills (e.g., *knowledge of ways and means of dealing with specifics, knowledge of the universals and abstractions in a field, translation, interpretation, extrapolation, application, analysis of organizational principles,* and *synthesis*) can be related to affective elements (e.g., *preference for* and *conceptualization of a value*):

I. You are planning to visit the Metropolitan Museum of Art and some friends of yours have asked you to select a reproduction of a work by a famous artist which suits their individual tastes. Indicate which artist's work you would select to fit each of your friend's tastes as represented in the statements below:

Key: A—a work by Goya
B—a work by Picasso
C—a work by Van Gogh
D—a work by Cézanne
E—a work by Dali

__C__ 1. "I can't remember the artist's name, but I was tremendously moved by the bright, bold, contrasting colors—so deeply expressive—with swirling, twisting, gyrating linear patterns in his landscapes and still lifes. His work seemed to be intoxicating."

__B__ 2. "I like modern art, but I much prefer art that has recognizable shapes and patterns of planes woven into articulate design and in contrasting colors. In other words, I like abstract designs when they reveal recognizable shapes, even though these shapes are not natural and are in unusual combinations—even flat in appearance."

  A   3. "I saw some etchings in the museum that were starkly realistic and powerful with irony and cynicism. My girl friend said the etchings were too caustic for her tastes, but I am really moved by such art."

  E   4. "Some time ago, I came across a magazine article showing some paintings by an artist who mingled recognizable objects and shapes in the most unusual ways—almost pictorial, but writhing, distorted, and convulsive—like the kinds of things that one might envision in a bad dream. Yet I really enjoyed the paintings because they made me conscious of our subconscious forces. While the paintings seemed almost cultlike, I found them fascinating."

II. A. In a paragraph, express your preference for the work of any artist whom we have studied, and identify the artist. (Be sure to explain *why* you prefer the given work.)

 B. Would you like to learn more about the personal life of an artist whom we have studied?

   Yes ————, No ————, Name of artist ————————.

III. A. From our study of urban architecture, name an office building that matches each of the following statements?

   1. "An office building is a machine to make money with." ——

   —————————————————————————————————

   2. "An office building is built for people, and therefore should be an aesthetically pleasing work of art." ————————————.

 B. Which of the preceding two opposing views do you support, and what arguments can you offer to convince the other party to change his view?

A group of items, applicable to English and the social studies, illustrates how cognitive outcomes (e.g., *knowledge of ways and means of dealing with specifics, interpretation, application, analysis of elements and relationships, synthesis,* and *evaluation*) can be evaluated along with affective outcomes (*preference for and conceptualization of a value*):

> Read the following quotation from the lead (cover) story of a national news magazine (*Newsweek,* November 6, 1967, p. 29) concerning a candidate for the office of Mayor of Boston:
>
> > They looked like characters right out of Moon Mullins, and she was their homegrown Mamie-made-good. Sloshing beer at the long tables in the unadorned main room of the South Boston Social and Athletic Club sat a comic-strip gallery of tipplers and brawlers and their tinseled, over-dressed dolls, and before them stood the belle of the evening, Louise Day Hicks. Her formidable 5 feet 10 inches and 175-odd pounds encased in a shimmering kelly-green suit, she planted herself stoutly before the microphone and spoke up in an unexpectedly small voice: "I seek this office in order to bring about change. . . . The greatest issue of all is that we feel alienated. No one in City Hall listens to us."
> >
> > And with those high-pitched words, the backlash had come of age. In a

firm but faintly singsong monotone, she transmitted her signal of fear and frustration to the solar plexus of the all-white gathering: it was time for beleaguered whites to reverse the eroding pressures from black slums. The same call to arms was reverberating ominously through many of the segregated central cities of America last week, but nowhere was it echoing with quite the clarion sophistication of Louise Day Hicks's crusade in the back streets of Boston.

"You know where I stand" is her theme, and probably the Statue of Liberty is the only other woman in the land who could say so with quite the same ironclad assurance that her meaning was precisely understood. Her fans love it. After Mrs. Hicks finished reading off her familiar recitation of civic wrongs the other night . . . a plinky-plink piano and banjo duet stomped into "Every little breeze seems to whisper" you-know-who— and the men queued up to give Louise their best, unscrewing cigar butts from their chins to buss her noisily on the cheek, or pumping her arm as if it were a jack handle under a trailer truck.

All the evening lacked was a bravo and a bouquet to make it a triumph. For unlikely as it may seem to outsiders, the large lady with the Helen Hokinson form and the grade-school delivery has become the sweetheart and savior-designate of the city's bypassed "little people," from South Boston's insular Irish to the Italian provincials of East Boston and the North End.

1. Underline every charged or loaded word and phrase in the preceding news story.
2. Assume that you are the reporter covering the preceding event. Rewrite the item so that it is slanted to create a favorable impression of the candidate. You are free to use any *charged* or *loaded* words and phrases, but you should not go beyond the facts presented in the original item.
3. Underline every *charged* or *loaded* word and phrase that you have used in rewriting the news item.

The foregoing group of items also shows how cognitive skills can be applied toward creating a better understanding of how language is used to influence attitudes, and how attitudes (and bias), expressed in language, can be used to color and distort the reader's interpretation of so-called factual events.

Essay-type items also can be useful in stimulating students to analyze and express attitudes, opinions, beliefs, and values in relation to cognitive learning. Although the essay-type item may not be the most efficient way of measuring the recall of information, it is an important means of encouraging the student to organize and express his ideas effectively. However, to avoid misinterpretation and to improve the reliability of such items, the teacher must see to it that they have some structure and specificity, and that criteria are established in advance for evaluating the answers. At the same time, the items, must allow sufficient leeway for the student to express his own ideas. In evaluating the essay-type item it also is important for the teacher to be open to divergent thinking, unanticipated insights, and other unanticipated patterns of thought that are appropriate to the question but do not fit the estabished criteria. In such cases the teacher may decide to revise the criteria so that students are given due credit for such responses.

The following is an example of an essay exercise that requires the student to interpret the attitudes and values expressed by an author in terms of the student's own background knowledge of specific developments while also allowing the student to express his own attitudes, opinions, and values:

> The following passage relates the experiences of a noted American composer when he was a young student of music in Paris in 1921:

>> Before the summer was very far advanced, rumors began to circulate of the presence at school of a brilliant harmony teacher, a certain Nadia Boulanger. . . . It took a considerable amount of persuasion on the part of a fellow student before I consented to "look in" on Mlle. Boulanger's class. On that particular day she was explaining the harmonic structure of one of the scenes from *Boris Godounoff*. I had never before witnessed such enthusiasm and such clarity in teaching. I immediately suspected that I had found my teacher.

>> There were several mental hurdles to get over first, however. No one to my knowledge had ever before thought of studying composition with a woman. The idea was absurd on the face of it. Everyone knows that the world has never produced a first-rate woman composer, so it follows that no woman could possibly hope to teach composition. Moreover, how would it sound to the folks back home? The whole idea was just a bit too revolutionary.

>> Nevertheless, and despite these excellent reasons, I visited Mlle. Boulanger in the fall and asked her to accept me as her pupil.[19]

> Discuss the implications of the foregoing passage with reference to
>   a. this historic development of woman's suffrage in the United States.
>   b. discrimination against women today.
>   c. the "women's liberation movement" of the 1970's.
>   d. the contributions of women in literature, science, and politics.
>   e. your own attitudes and opinions toward women's rights and responsibilities in society today (supported by appropriate citations or data).

The preceding exercise, appropriately modified, also can be used as a basis for a variety of related library assignments, themes, panel presentations and discussions, and other learning activities.

A similar essay exercise, following, illustrates the use of a factual statement to introduce the student to a problem of great social significance and controversy. Again, the student is required not only to demonstrate his knowledge and understandings of the possible measures to be taken by society in dealing with the problem, but also his own attitudes, opinions, and even values relating to the problem.

---

[19] Aaron Copland, *Our New Music* (New York: Whittlesey House, 1941), pp. 218–219.

As recently as 1920, our nation's population was 100 million. In 1967 we added another 100 million. If American families average three children, and if there is no increase in immigration, our population will soar to 321 million by the year 2000 and to nearly a billion a hundred years from now. Biologists tell us that the control of human births remains the primary human problem. Yet, in recent years, our federal government has allocated for the space program alone about 35 times the funds allocated for population programs.

1. What are the chief measures that have been proposed for controlling the human population?
2. What nonbiological objections have been raised in opposition to certain proposed measures for controlling the human population, and what are *your* opinions concerning these measures?

Again, the student is free to express his own opinion, attitudes, and values in the second part of the preceding exercise, but he is required to relate these affective considerations to specific social, political, ethical, and religious positions. He is evaluated according to his awareness and understanding of these positions, not according to the side he takes on each issue.

THE AFFECTIVE TAXONOMY—PROBLEMS AND CRITICISMS

Although affective goals are commonly found in broad educational statements and, more recently, in materials connected with the modern curriculum reform projects, the instruments and procedures for evaluating learning tend to be directed almost exclusively toward assessing cognitive outcomes. Krathwohl, Bloom, and Masia found that where the original statements for new courses frequently appear to give as much emphasis to affective objectives as to cognitive objectives, there tends to be a "rapid dropping of the affective objectives from the statements about the course and an almost complete disappearance of efforts at appraisal of student growth in this domain." [20]

Some of the chief reasons for this neglect are (1) the failure of teachers and curriculum specialists to appreciate fully the necessary interrelationships and interdependence between affective and cognitive objectives; (2) the concentration on cognitive learnings in the curriculum reform projects of the 1950's and 1960's; (3) the emphasis on cognitive learnings (particularly those at the lower levels of the taxonomy) in traditional schooling—coupled with the long-held concept of mind as an entity separate from the emotions, along with the persistent, time-worn belief that the mind is best strengthened through rigorous "intellective exercise"; (4) the new emphasis on operant conditioning and the treatment of the learner as an automatic mechanism; (5) the enormous difficulty inherent in teaching for and evaluating affective learning in conjunction with

---

[20] Krathwohl, Bloom, and Masia, op. cit., p. 16.

cognitive learning; and (6) the controversies attached to evaluating attitudes, feelings, emotions, and values. A brief review of some of these factors should help illustrate the difficulties connected with the evaluation of affective outcomes.

Failure to Appreciate the Interdependence of Cognitive and Affective Objectives

In Part I of this book, and earlier in Part II, emphasis was given to the necessary interrelationships and interdependence between affective and cognitive objectives. In the classification schema or taxonomy for affective objectives just presented, it is seen that the first level or category is *receiving.* Obviously no cognitive learning can take place unless the student is receptive. At the most elemental level, he must be *aware* of a given condition, phenomenon, situation, or problem in the learning environment. His *willingness to receive,* or his receptiveness, varies from mere acquiescence to eagerness, from dissatisfaction to satisfaction. This can be considered as an important aspect of motivation. Moreover, whether a student is eager to learn because he seeks a high grade, or because he is vitally interested in the subject matter, can have a decisive influence on the cognitive learning outcomes. The next level in receiving, *controlled or selected attention,* denotes the student's behavior in perceiving more specifically the elements or components in the learning situation.

Similarly, the act of *responding* is necessary for cognitive learning. Here too the responses may vary from mere acquiescence to eagerness, from dissatisfaction to satisfaction. And as in the case of *receiving,* the qualities of the response, or the motives underlying the response, have important bearings on the character and outcomes of the learning experience.

The third level of the affective taxonomy, *valuing,* also has important influences on cognitive learning, although this is considerably more difficult to demonstrate, because *valuing* is a process that is developed over a long term. Nevertheless, when students are investigating many controversial issues, their cognitive styles are influenced by their values and vice versa. For example, the adolescent's views on such topics as environmental pollution, narcotics, war, dress codes, racial inequities, rights of protest, and social status cannot be derived through cognitive learning in the absence of affective learning. Moreover, how a student selects and interprets data or evidence is influenced by his interests, attitudes, feelings, emotions, and values.

Although not many educators today would deny the importance of affective learnings in the process of education, such learnings have been and continue to be neglected in our schools. Surprisingly few educators, including those responsible for the major curriculum reform projects, have given adequate attention to the vital relationship and organic interdependence of affective and cognitive learning.

Curriculum Reform Projects
and Affective Learning

The cold war period of the 1950's and 1960's was marked by an unprecedented surge of curriculum reform projects concentrated on the specialized disciplines. Capping the cold war syndrome was the dramatic space race, creating a new urgency in the pursuit of intellectual excellence. Although it is not the purpose of this book to treat these developments and their influences on the curriculum in any great detail, the point to be emphasized here is that key focus in the curriculum reform efforts during this period was on the development of high-powered styles of cognitive learning, from the primary grades through the university.

Pursuit of Intellectual Excellence. As Jerome Bruner noted in his introduction to the report of the Woods Hole Conference (held in September 1959—less than a year after Sputnik I—under the auspices of the National Academy of Sciences), "What may be emerging as a mark of our own generation is a widespread renewal of concern for the quality and intellectual aims of education . . . accentuated by what is almost certain to be a long-range crisis in national security." [21]

Through funds from the National Science Foundation, new courses were produced by teams of university scholars representing the specialized disciplines and focusing on "disciplined inquiry"—the style of the scholar-specialist at work. A basic thesis underlying the leading curriculum projects was that intellectual activity anywhere is the same, regardless of whether the individual is a leading scientist or a third grader. [22]

Oddly, the ancient conception of the child as a miniature adult was reborn. Moreover, the thesis that "intellectual activity anywhere is the same" was so totally and vigorously embraced by the scholar-specialists responsible for the new curriculum reforms that insufficient attention was given to the necessary relationships between affective and cognitive learning. For the time being, the scholar-specialists seemed to have forgotten that adolescents are interested in the applications of knowledge and that achievement and career goals are influenced by interests, attitudes, feelings, and values, and not by force-fed cognitive styles.

Unanticipated Outcomes and Alternative Strategies. Discussed at the beginning of Part II was the unexpected decline in the proportion of students taking high school physics following the widespread adoption of the PSSC physics course. In recognizing the neglect both of affective goals and the practical applications of knowledge in the PSSC course, Harvard Project Physics was established

---

[21] Jerome S. Bruner, *The Process of Education* (Cambridge, Mass.: Harvard University Press, 1960), p. 1.

[22] Ibid., p. 14.

with the claim that it represented a "new emphasis" by relating the subject to "the beautiful and sometimes awesome story of how real people made physics," and in "attempting to provide high school students with an exciting course treating fundamental physical ideas in a humane context." [23] The use of the terms *beautiful, awesome, exciting,* and *humane* is vivid testimony to the recognition, on the part of the developers of this course, of the need to make the subject matter meaningful to the high school student on a "personal" level. In this connection the developers of Harvard Project Physics note that in the past, "references to scientists have been too closely tied to the published digest of their scientific contributions, while insufficient attention has been given to their personalities and living patterns." [24] Thus, unlike the PSSC course, Harvard Project Physics was designed to emphasize the personal and sociological aspects of physics by relating the central ideas of the discipline to applications in the practical world. A notable aspect of Harvard Project Physics has been the effort to assay student satisfactions with the course.

Nevertheless, the problem of developing the content of the alternative course so as to accommodate both affective and cognitive objectives is yet to be solved. For example, a review of the actual questions and problems which appear in the student text for Harvard Project Physics reveals that although there has been a notable effort to make the items interesting, the items are geared almost entirely to cognitive learnings.[25] On the other hand, the supplementary reading material and films developed for the course are impressive in the emphasis given to the personal and sociological aspects of physics.

Changing Ends and Means. In the social studies the major curriculum reform efforts during the 1950's and 1960's were patterned largely after the prestigious discipline-centered science projects. Moreover, many social scientists held that the high school should redirect the curriculum in the social studies away from "desirable sociocivic objectives" and toward the discipline-centered goal of university scholars who see their specialties as leading toward "a science of human behavior." In the words of a sociologist, "nothing but confusion can result from equating the objective study of society with a means for securing the good life." [26]

Although most of the curriculum reform projects in the social studies during the 1950's and 1960's were designed to accommodate the discipline-centered interests of university scholar-specialists, a notable exception was the issue-

---

23 Harvard Project Physics, *Harvard Project Physics Progress Report* (Cambridge, Mass.: The Project, 1967), pp. 10, 31.

24 Ibid., p. 52.

25 See *The Project Physics Course Text* (New York: Holt, Rinehart and Winston, Inc., 1970).

26 Gresham M. Sykes, "Sociology," in American Council of Learned Societies and the National Council for the Social Studies, *The Social Studies and the Social Sciences* (New York: Harcourt Brace Jovanovich, Inc., 1962), p. 159.

centered approach developed by Oliver and Shaver.[27] One of the important goals of this approach is to enable the learner to understand how values and value conflicts relate to public issues. In developing the issue-centered or juris-prudential approach, Oliver and Shaver emphasize that their work "is meant to be an open challenge to current efforts to redefine the social studies in narrow academic terms." [28] They go on to advocate that "attitudinal and temperamental, as well as intellectual, dimensions (should) run through the objectives of any social studies program," because the student "brings to the instructional setting a fairly stable set of interrelated personal constructs which affect how he reacts, both emotionally and intellectually, to personal and social events." [29]

These efforts by Oliver and Shaver during the mid-1960's represented a protest against the prevailing discipline-centered projects and the neglect of the affective learnings that are so crucial in shaping thought and action. During the late 1960's the growing student demands for curriculum "relevance" were joined by radical critics calling for more humanized schooling. This caused many specialists in the social sciences and other fields to give renewed attention to the need for reorganizing their subject matter so that more direct treatment might be devoted to pervading social problems and issues, and to affective learning outcomes.[30]

The Persistent Doctrine of Mental Discipline

The notion of a mind–body dualism, held by Plato and Aristotle, not only came to be supported by religious orthodoxy (which conceived of mind as the spiritual link between God and man), but came to exert enormous influence on the curriculum through most of the nineteenth century as a result of faculty psychology. The faculty psychologists contended that the mind consisted of separate sets of faculties—the intellect, the emotions or feelings, and the will or volition.

This conception of mind came to be embraced by many leading educators of the nineteenth century who held that the central task of education is to discipline the mind. And what could be more effective for mental discipline than the time-honored classical studies or "liberal arts"—as opposed to the practical and newly emerging scientific studies? By concentrating on exercising the intellective or cognitive faculty of mind through drill work in the most rigorous studies, however distasteful, the learner's powers of reason could best be strengthened. Such strengthening, it was contended, would endow the learner

---

[27] Donald W. Oliver and James P. Shaver, *Teaching Public Issues in High School* (Boston: Houghton Mifflin Company, 1966).

[28] Ibid., p. xii.

[29] Ibid., p. 232.

[30] See Morris Janowitz, *Institution Building in Urban Education* (New York: Russell Sage Foundation, 1966), pp. 47–60.

with transfer powers to subsequent mental tasks in virtually any intellective area.

Emerging Criticism. The biologist Thomas Henry Huxley, a supporter of Darwin, ridiculed the doctrine of mental discipline in an essay written in 1868 and later published in a volume of essays on science and education.

> It is wonderful how close a parallel to classical training could be made out of that paleontology to which I refer. In the first place I could get up an osteological primer so arid, so pedantic in its terminology, so altogether distasteful to the youthful mind, as to beat the recent famous production of the headmasters out of the field in all these excellences. Next, I could exercise my boys upon early fossils, and bring out all their powers of memory and all their ingenuity in the application of my osteo-grammatical rules to the interpretation, or construing, of these fragments. . . . That would answer to verse-making and essay-writing in the dead languages.[31]

With the emergence of other schools of psychology and the experimental research on learning during the early years of the twentieth century, along with the influences of Freud and Dewey, the doctrine of mental discipline came to be discredited. But it was far from being demolished as far as educational practice was concerned. In making the case that "we are dealing with human minds, and not with dead matter," [32] Whitehead offered this condemnation of the doctrine of mental discipline:

> I appeal to you, as practical teachers. With good discipline, it is always possible to pump into the minds of a class a certain quantity of inert knowledge. . . . The child then knows how to solve a quadratic equation. But what is the point of teaching a child to solve a quadratic equation? There is a traditional answer to this question. It runs thus: The mind is an instrument, you first sharpen it, and then use it; the acquisition of the power of solving a quadratic equation is part of the process of sharpening the mind. Now there is just enough truth in this answer to have made it live through the ages. But for all its half-truth, it embodies a radical error which bids fair to stifle the genius of the modern world. I do not know who was first responsible for this analogy of the mind to a dead instrument. For aught I know, it may have been one of the seven wise men of Greece, or a committee of the whole lot of them. Whoever was the originator, there can be no doubt of the authority which it has acquired by the continuous approval bestowed upon it by eminent persons. But whatever its weight of authority, whatever the high approval which it can quote, I have no hesitation in denouncing it as one of the most fatal, erroneous, and dangerous conceptions ever introduced into the theory of education.[33]

---

[31] Thomas H. Huxley, *Science and Education: Essays,* "A Liberal Education; and Where to Find It" (New York: Appleton-Century-Crofts, Inc., 1897), pp. 98–99.
[32] Whitehead, op. cit., p. 8.
[33] Ibid., pp. 8–9.

Whitehead argued that the life of the mind cannot be postponed until after it has been "sharpened," for "education is the acquisition of the art of the utilisation of knowledge." [34]

In attacking the traditional dogma of mind–body dualism, Dewey observed that remnants of this dualism are found in contemporary education where "there is the unquestioned assumption of 'faculties' to be trained, and . . . there is comparative disregard of the earth on which men happen to live and the bodies they happen to carry around with them." [35] The newer findings in the psychology of learning, coupled with the rising social consciousness during the era of progressive education, gave support to curriculum diversification to meet the emerging demands of science and technology. At the same time, the need for curriculum synthesis and coherence was emphasized by progressive educators in the light of the expansion and diversification of the curriculum, the recognition that massive learning transfer does not occur automatically from one field to another, and the growing awareness of the need for common learnings to serve as the social cement of a nation composed of people of diverse national and cultural origins. At the same time, the changing conception of man required a new pedagogical orientation—one that would give attention to the feelings, needs, interests, and motivations of the learner.

Essentialism and the Revival of Mental Discipline. The advent of the cold war at mid-century produced a severe reaction to the progressive movement. Leading critics of progressive education advocated that our schools concentrate mainly on the traditional studies that are necessary for training the mind. Soon after Sputnik I, Rickover had this to say regarding the responsibility of the school to concern itself solely with the mind:

> For all children, the educational process must be one of collecting factual knowledge to the limit of their absorptive capacity . . . and it is with the mind that the school must solely concern itself. . . . To acquire such knowledge, fact upon fact, takes time and effort. Nothing can really make it "fun." [36]

Rickover's rationale not only conceives of mind as a sponge or vessel, to be filled with factual knowledge, but negates the importance of affective influences on academic achievement. The implication of Rickover's position is that if school learning is to train the mind, such learning must be made very difficult for, if not distasteful to, the learner. The view that "nothing can really make it (learning) 'fun' " rejects the possibility that students can engender enthusiasm and enjoyment in learning.

In his Pulitzer Prize-winning book, Richard Hofstadter labeled progressive education as "life-adjustment education" and linked this brand of pedagogy

---

34 Ibid., p. 6.

35 Dewey, *Democracy and Education,* op. cit., p. 287.

36 Hyman G. Rickover, "European vs. American Secondary Schools," *Phi Delta Kappan,* Vol. 40 (November, 1958), p. 61.

with the anti-intellectual forces in American life.[37] Hofstadter contended that the doctrine of mental discipline and the notion of transfer had been discredited by the "life-adjusters" through the "misuse of experimental evidence" and that this misuse "constitutes a major scandal in the history of educational thought."[38] Hofstadter cited Bruner's statement that "virtually all of the evidence of the last two decades on the nature of learning and transfer has indicated that . . . it is indeed a fact that massive general transfer can be achieved by appropriate learning, even to the degree that learning properly under optimum conditions leads one 'to learn how to learn.'"[39] However, in stating the case for mental discipline and transfer, Hofstadter ignored Bruner's qualification that "transfer can be achieved by *appropriate* learning." Moreover, Hofstadter failed to consider Bruner's concommitant requisite of "learning how to learn" if general massive transfer is to be effected. The importance of "learning how to learn" is derived in no small measure from Dewey's "reflective thinking" and Dewey's rejection of the time-worn notion of mind as an instrument to be sharpened through meaningless drill.

The Automatic Learner

The theory of operant conditioning, derived from behaviorism and based upon laboratory experiments with rats and pigeons, attracted a considerable number of adherents during the 1950's and 1960's as a result of developments in educational technology and the support of research and demonstration projects through federal and private foundation funds.

Although the theory of operant conditioning rejects the notion of dualism between mind and body, it reduces human learning to a process of reinforcement or of forming connections between stimuli and responses through repetitive tasks that are measured in terms of overt behavior.[40] Appropriate terminal "behaviors" or responses are carefully specified, and these responses are elicited and made automatic through programmed instruction and the needed technological media.

Learner as Mechanism. Thus the learner is treated as a simple mechanism to be conditioned in a manner so that the desired responses are automatic. According to Skinner, many of the effects that are traditionally considered matters of motivation actually are, in principal operation, "simply the arrangement of contingencies of reinforcement."[41] In other words, the diligent and eager student behaves as he does "not because he . . . has a positive attitude toward his

---

[37] Richard Hofstadter, *Anti-intellectualism in American Life* (New York: Alfred A. Knopf, Inc., 1963), Chapter 13.

[38] Ibid., p. 349.

[39] Bruner, op. cit., p. 6.

[40] See B. F. Skinner, *The Technology of Teaching* (New York: Appleton-Century-Crofts, 1968).

[41] Ibid., p. 11.

education, but because he has been exposed to effective contingencies of reinforcement." [42] Even creative or original work—as well as such desirable qualities as interest, enthusiasm, and dedication—is simply a matter of building the proper repertoire of contingencies of reinforcement, according to the behaviorist.

> The poet's metaphor and the scientist's analogy are often far fetched, and how far they are fetched depends in part on the contingencies of reinforcement which breed interest, enthusiasm, and dedication. A powerful technology of teaching can strengthen these sources of originality—in any number of students.[43]

Consequently, the behaviorist regards purpose in the same mechanical way as any other kind of human activity, and desirable learning activity is simply a matter of eliciting the necessary reactive behaviors through operant conditioning. Such a mechanistic conception of the learner, according to the noted novelist Arthur Koestler, serves to deny the existence of qualities which account for the "humanity of man" as contrasted with the "rattiness of the rat." [44] Affective aspects of the teaching–learning process are reduced to a mechanical formula and need no special consideration beyond reinforcement contingencies.

Limited Influences. Not surprisingly, then, the heightened interest in programmed instruction and its concommitant technology during the decades of the 1950's and 1960's was accompanied by the tendency to subordinate affective learning to cognitive learning.

However, despite the enormous financial support for the new technology, provided by the federal government and the private foundations, the predicted revolution in teaching has not come to pass. Programmed instruction is as tedious, repetitious, and boring as are the traditional modes of classroom instruction and drill. Research studies have failed to demonstrate the superiority of programmed instruction over the "less efficient" traditional methods. And as we entered the decade of the 1970's, social critics and student activists were advocating that our schools become more humanizing. Accordingly, education should not be concerned merely with imparting knowledge of "what is," but should be engaged in applying knowledge and values in terms of "what should be" for a better society. Instead of being "under control," the learner must be "in control" of the forces which influence his destiny.

Behavioral Objectives and Specifications

In Part I we discussed the narrow and mechanistic viewpoint taken by some of the leading proponents of behavioral objectives who hold that "the only

---

42 Ibid., p. 160.

43 Ibid., p. 183.

44 Arthur Koestler, *The Ghost in the Machine* (New York: The Macmillan Company, 1967), p. 15.

sensible reason for the educator's engaging in instruction is to modify the learner's behavior; therefore, these intended changes must be described in terms of measurable learner behaviors." [45] However, in Part I it was noted not only that some of the most significant learning outcomes defy existing measures of quantification, but that the actual quantification of such outcomes may prove to be destructive. Thus, for example, one can learn a great deal about the anatomy and physiology of the frog through dissection, but in the process the frog is killed, and there is no way to bring the poor creature back to life.

Learning and Life. Some of the most complex forms of human behavior, such as learning oral communication, occur in the absence of formal instruction. The child learns such behavior through emulation of other humans and via observation and interaction in real-life situational contexts. To dissect such processes into behavioral fragments may well destroy the qualities which make such learning a living experience. This does not mean that formal and systematic instruction can be dispensed with. As a designed environment, the school makes possible all kinds of learning that could not be gotten through chance experience in society. No modern technological society has demonstrated that it can do without schools.

The great irony is that most statements of behavioral specifications, because they must be reduced to measurable or quantifiable units, are far from being *behaviors* in the real-life sense. Dewey noted that "in the degree in which what is communicated cannot be organized into the existing experience of the learner, it becomes *mere* words: that is, pure sense-stimuli, lacking in meaning. Then it operates to call out mechanical reactions. . . ." [46]

Limitations of Specifications. Efforts to develop cognitive and affective taxonomies of educational objectives have been followed by the insistence on the part of some educators that in order to determine instructional adequacy, "the instructor must clearly specify his objectives in terms of measurable learner behavior." [47] Not only does this emasculate teaching of its artistic quality, but it implies that unless qualitative aspects of teaching and learning are reduced to quantifiable measures, teachers are deluding themselves and their students with fictions. As in the fable by Hans Christian Anderson, the princess and her court were readily able to convince themselves of the superiority of the artificial rose over the real rose, because the real rose could not measure up to the artificial one in terms of the criterion of durability.

The problem with excessive insistence on building specifications for each and every educational objective is that human beings are not built like auto-

45 W. James Popham et al., in *Instructional Objectives* (Chicago: Rand McNally & Company, 1969), p. 35.

46 Dewey, *Democracy and Education,* op. cit., p. 221.

47 Popham, op. cit., p. 39.

mobiles or washing machines. The consequence of such detailed specifications in education is that "achievement comes to denote the sort of thing that a well-planned machine can do better than a human being can, and the main effect of education, the achieving of a life of rich significance, drops by the wayside." [48]

As an outgrowth of programmed instruction, behavioral specifications are intended to remove the uncertainty of outcomes of the teaching–learning process. Yet without the uncertainty element, learning is not much of an adventure.

The affective and cognitive taxonomies can be useful instruments in enabling the teacher to emphasize styles of thinking other than recall and to develop a coherent relationship between affective influences and cognitive outcomes. Interpreted too literally and mechanistically, the taxonomies can lose much of their vitality and value.

The Evaluation Controversy

Should students be graded according to achievement on affective objectives? Earlier in Part II, a differentiation was made between tests that are designed primarily to evaluate affective outcomes and tests that are intended to be used in assessing affective learning as integrally related to cognitive learning. In either case, however, the evaluation of affective outcomes is intended for diagnostic and feedback purposes rather than for grading. Even where tests are designed to assess affective outcomes in direct relation to cognitive outcomes, the common practice is to assign grades according to cognitive, not affective, achievement.

Formative and Summative Evaluation. Bloom, Hastings, and Madaus hold that "although it may not be a good practice to assign a summative grade for affective behavior, it is often desirable to evaluate a student's affective behavior formatively." [49] Here the use of the term *summative* refers to assigning a grade for student achievement at the end of a term, course, or instructional program, whereas the term *formative* denotes the on-going or systematic assessment of student achievement while the term, course, or instructional program is in progress. Bloom, Hastings, and Madaus hold that "feedback to the student, not the assignment of a grade, should be the purpose of making a formative evaluation of affective objectives." [50]

On the other hand, although acknowledging the inherent difficulties in grading students on affective achievement in comparison to cognitive achievement, an earlier statement by Krathwohl, Bloom, and Masia holds that these difficulties and technical problems probably can be solved if sufficient effort is put to

[48] Dewey, *Democracy and Education,* op. cit., p. 277.
[49] Bloom, Hastings, and Madaus, op. cit., p. 227.
[50] Ibid.

the task.[51] They illustrate their case with an affective objective calling for "the development of the ability to become sensitive to and perceptive of different aspects of a musical work," and point out that a student can be graded on such an objective by presenting him with a series of unfamiliar musical compositions and having him respond to questions that are designed to reveal the elements that he is capable of perceiving.[52] In actual practice, however, such test items tend to be used in evaluating cognitive outcomes primarily, although these items also can be directed at affective outcomes. In other words, even in a class in music or art *appreciation,* the tests employed in assigning grades tend to be directed at the assessment of cognitive outcomes and affective outcomes are given relatively little emphasis.

Although it is clear that instruments for assessing cognitive achievement can and should engage the learner in an affectively positive way by being interesting, challenging, encouraging, and satisfying, there is considerable doubt as to whether it is desirable to assign grades to students on so-called purely affective measures. Not only do many educators believe that a student should not be graded on his attitudes and values, but they believe that such grading would likely lead the student to falsify his responses in order to attain a good grade. This does not imply that assessment of affective learnings should be avoided. Such assessment is of vital importance in improving a course or curriculum.

Organic Relationship. Equally important is the need for educators to recognize the organic relationship between the cognitive and affective processes. Because these processes are virtually inseparable, efforts need to be made to incorporate affective with cognitive objectives in assessing student achievement. As illustrated in the test items earlier in Part II, if a learner is responding to a significant social or political issue, or to a question of preference in music or art, or to a controversial problem in biology, his attitudes undoubtedly will influence his cognitive processes and vice versa. For example, there would be no such thing as a controversial issue in the absence of conflicting *opinions.* And *opinions* are not formed through cognitive learning alone. Experiences in the home, community, and school all serve to shape attitudes, feelings, and values which, in turn, influence how one forms opinions on controversial matters. These affective forces also determine in no small measure whether one is open- or closed-minded to viewpoints and evidence that conflict with one's own outlook, just as they influence how one goes about selecting and interpreting data on a controversial matter. To assume that the curriculum and the means of evaluation should be limited to cognitive goals may well be self-defeating, because such an assumption ignores the necessary interaction between affective and cognitive learning. "There is only one alternative to value-directed and value-affecting teaching in the social studies and related areas," maintains

---

[51] Krathwohl, Bloom, and Masia, op. cit., p. 17.
[52] Ibid.

Scriven, "and that is not just cowardice but *incompetence, professional* incompetence." [53]

Guidelines. In dealing with values, as in dealing with any curriculum content, indoctrination is to be avoided by following these guidelines:

1. We teach as facts only those assertions which really can be objectively established . . . ; others we teach as hypotheses. Hence, we do not violate the rights of others to make their own choices where choice is rationally possible, nor their right to know the truth where it is known.
2. Good teaching does not consist primarily in requiring the memorization of conclusions that the teacher thinks are true, but in developing the skills needed to arrive at and test conclusions. . . . it is a moral obligation (as well as a pragmatic one) not to force on others views which they are given no chance to assess.
3. That certain conclusions should now be treated as established does not mean they can ever turn out to be wrong. . . . [54]

If educators choose to ignore affective learning, the student is left with a limited and misleading conception of how knowledge is developed and used in solving problems. For example, two leading historians or economists may differ sharply in their interpretations of certain events or conditions as a result of differences in their sociopolitical outlooks, despite the fact that they have equal access to the same sources of data. How they go about interpreting data is ultimately related to their attitudes, emotions, sociopolitical backgrounds and dispositions, and life outlook.

By ignoring or avoiding the assessment of affective outcomes, not only do educators deny themselves opportunities to improve the curriculum, but there is the real danger that "the development of cognitive behaviors may actually destroy certain desired affective behaviors and that instead of a positive relation between growth in cognitive and affective behavior . . . there may be an inverse relation between growth in the two domains." [55]

Affective Assessment and the Assault on Privacy

There is an essential difference between evaluating affective outcomes as discussed in these pages and evaluating personality factors that are associated with "personal privacy." In recent years, for example, there has been a marked increase in the use of personality tests through which job applicants are scrutinized on their personal beliefs, values, and behaviors. The applicant's scores on various personality measures are used to determine whether he is a desirable

53 Michael Scriven, "Student Values as Educational Objectives," in *Proceedings of the 1965 Invitational Conference on Testing Problems* (Princeton, N.J.: Educational Testing Service, 1966), p. 42.

54 Ibid., pp. 44–45.

55 Krathwohl, Bloom, and Masia, op. cit., p. 20.

or undesirable prospect. Where many adults soon learn how to respond to the "right-think" items, adolescents and children may be more vulnerable because they are more candid and less test-wise.

Aside from the questionable validity of many standardized personality tests, most of these instruments are scored and interpreted in terms of desirable and undesirable weightings; consequently, the wise test taker learns that he must conform to the established norms. Not only do such uses of these instruments breed for conformity, but they often constitute an invasion of personal privacy. Such conformity is contrary to what education stands for in a free society, and such invasion of personal privacy should be beyond the province of the teacher.

It is one thing for the school to enable youngsters to investigate all sides of important controversial topics, such as racism, crime prevention and control, environmental pollution, or the military–industrial complex. The school must avoid indoctrination and "right-think" where opinions, attitudes, and values are concerned. Enlightenment is a product of choice, not indoctrination. It is quite another thing for the school to attempt to gauge the personality attributes of its students through tests that are comprised of such ridiculously forced and prying questions as, "Do you think Jesus Christ was a greater man than Abraham Lincoln?" [56]

There is an essential difference between using a problem inventory as one means of helping to determine the kinds of problems that might be included in a problems of democracy course and employing a test to score a student on such forced and artificially dichotomized personality attributes as practical versus imaginative, placid versus apprehensive, group-dependent versus self-sufficient, and so on. Teachers need to understand the interests, needs, attitudes, motivations, and problems of their students. As emphasized throughout this book, cognitive learning is not independent of affective learning. Moreover, the school has a responsibility to refer students with serious problems of mal-adjustment to appropriate clinical specialists. But the school also has the responsibility to respect the personal privacy of youth.

Differences in attitudes, beliefs, and values can make the lesson come alive with controversy. And controversy can be a constructive force in the teaching–learning process, as well as in social problem solving, where the aim and function of schooling is the fostering of open-mindedness. As George Bernard Shaw observed, "controversy is education in itself; a controversially educated person with an open mind is better educated than a dogmatically educated one with a closed mind." [57]

---

[56] Robert Sherrill, "The Assault on Privacy," *The New York Times Book Review*, March 14, 1971, p. 3.

[57] George Bernard Shaw, *Doctor's Delusions, Crude Criminology, and Sham Education* (London: Constable, 1950), p. 314.

SUMMARY

Educators have not recognized the necessary interdependence of cognitive and affective processes in teaching and learning. Although lip-service is commonly given to the need to develop desirable attitudes, interests, motivations, and values in schooling, actual instructional and testing practices reveal an emphasis on cognitive outcomes almost to the exclusion of affective outcomes.

During the decade of the 1950's, influential essentialists were advocating that the school must concentrate on cultivating the intellect and must abandon its socializing functions. The crisis syndrome of the cold war resulted in a national drive for the pursuit of academic excellence. Essentialist critics revived the traditional notion of intellect as a force existing apart from feelings, emotions, or corporeal influences.

Essentialist criticism faded into the background, however, as the federally supported curriculum reform projects of the 1950's and 1960's transformed the national pursuit of academic excellence from a slogan to a mission. A fundamental doctrine undergirding the new curriculum reform projects was that "intellectual activity anywhere is the same," and the schoolboy learning something for the first time is undergoing the same kind of intellective experience as is the mature scholar-specialist who is probing into the far reaches of his discipline. Because the young learner was to be regarded as a miniature version of the mature scholar-specialist, the focus of attention in the educative process could be transferred from the nature of the learner to the nature of the academician. Affective goals and outcomes in the educative process could be shunted aside in favor of cognitive goals and outcomes.

However, during the late 1960's and the early 1970's, new voices were heard. Radical critics and student activists in our colleges and secondary schools were calling for curriculum "relevance" and humanized schooling. New curriculum projects, focusing on the applications of knowledge and seeking to relate affective learning to cognitive goals, began to emerge.

Nevertheless, despite these developments, efforts to evaluate affective outcomes of education have been far from fruitful. There is an adage that "students learn what they are tested and graded on." Because educators are unable to justify the grading of students on affective learning outcomes, the tendency is to continue to emphasize cognitive learning without giving sufficient attention to meeting important affective objectives in the educative process. The answer lies not in grading students on affective outcomes, but in recognizing the organic relationship between cognitive and affective processes. Curriculum improvement requires a recognition of this vital relationship, along with more meaningful measures for assessing new curricula in terms of both affective and cognitive changes in the learner. The method of intelligence requires a conscious awareness of how affective influences shape thought.

PROBLEMS FOR STUDY AND DISCUSSION

1. Dewey observed that intellectual growth is not possible "without an active disposition to welcome points of view hitherto alien." [John Dewey, *Democracy and Education* (New York: The Macmillan Company, 1916), p. 206.] How do you account for the tendency of many teachers to neglect and even to avoid topics that require an examination of differences in pupil attitudes, opinions, beliefs, and values?

2. A contemporary educational critic contends that existing practice "makes it clear to students that the purpose of testing is not evaluation but rating—to produce grades that enable the school to rank students and sort them in various ways for administrative purposes. The result is to destroy any interest in learning. . . ." [Charles E. Silberman, *Crisis in the Classroom* (New York: Random House, 1970), p. 348.] Do you agree with this statement? Explain.

3. Is it possible for tests to be used for the evaluation of learning and, at the same time, for the stimulation of interest in learning? How? If not, why not?

4. Many educators acknowledge that affective goals have not received adequate emphasis in the curriculum. How do you account for this?

5. The decades of the 1950's and 1960's were marked by what might be called the pursuit of academic excellence syndrome. Writing for the Council for Basic Education on school priorities for the 1960's, a school superintendent offered these comments:

   In short, if there is any domain in which excellence—and I do not mean mere competency but excellence—may be and should be, indeed must be, pursued by the American school, it does not lie . . . with well-adjusted needs, interests, and attitudes. Our aim in the schools must be cerebration, our domain chiefly, most chiefly, the mind. [William H. Cornog, "What Are the Priorities for the Public Schools in the 1960's?" Occasional Paper No. 5 (Washington, D.C.: Council for Basic Education, 1963), p. 1.]

   What are the educational implications of the preceding statement in the light of the conclusion reached by Piaget, one of the world's leading psychologists, that "we cannot reason, even in pure mathematics, without experiencing certain feelings, and conversely, no affect can exist without a minimum of understanding"? [Jean Piaget, *The Psychology of Intelligence* (1947), translated by M. Piercy and D. E. Derlyne (Paterson, N.J.: Little-field, Adams, and Company, 1960), p. 6.]

6. The author of the statement for the Council for Basic Education quoted in problem 5, above, goes on to express this viewpoint regarding individual differences?

   After thirty years or more in the business, I think I know something about individual differences. There *are* jugs of different capacity, and there are pourers of different capacity, too. What I am talking about here is the nature of the wine and its availability to all." [Cornog, op. cit., p. 3.]

Is the analogy of mind as a jug of a certain capacity valid? Why or why not? What are the implications of conceiving of the teacher's role as a "pourer" of wine (knowledge) into different-sized jugs (minds)?

7. During the late 1960's and early 1970's radical students were demanding that the curriculum in school and college should be overhauled so as to be made "relevant" to student interests. Fifty years ago Dewey had this to say about students' interests:

Interests in reality are but attitudes toward possible experiences; they are not achievements. . . . To take the phenomena presented at a given age as in any way self-explanatory or self-contained is inevitably to result in indulgence and spoiling. . . . Appealing to interest upon the present plane means excitation; it means playing with a power so as continually to stir it up without directing it toward definite achievement. Continuous initiation, continuous starting of activities that do not arrive is, for all practical purposes, as bad as the continual repression of initiative. . . . It is as if the child were forever tasting and never eating; always having his palate tickled upon the emotional side, but never getting the organic satisfaction that comes only with the digestion of food and transformation of it into working power. [John Dewey, *The Child and the Curriculum* (Chicago: The University of Chicago Press, 1902), pp. 15–16.]

Do you see any relationship between the demands of some radical students to be allowed to "do their own thing," and Dewey's criticism of education that regards the expression of interests by the learner as a proper and central end? Explain.

8. What significance does Dewey's statement, quoted in question 7, have for the responsibility of the teacher to relate interests to cognitive learning so as to generate "working power"?

9. What advantages, limitations, and/or dangers do you see in the position that teachers must specify and measure all instructional objectives?

SELECTED REFERENCES

Aylesworth, Thomas G., and Gerald M. Reagan. *Teaching for Thinking.* Garden City, N.Y.: Doubleday & Company, Inc., 1969.

Beatty, Walcott H. (ed.). *Improving Educational Assessment & an Inventory of Measures of Affective Behavior.* Washington, D.C.: Association for Supervision and Curriculum Development, NEA, 1969.

Berg, Harry D. (ed.). *Evaluation in Social Studies.* Thirty-fifth Yearbook. Washington, D.C.: National Council for the Social Studies, 1965.

Bloom, Benjamin S. (ed.). *Taxonomy of Educational Objectives, Handbook I: Cognitive Domain.* New York: David McKay Company, Inc., 1956.

Bloom, Benjamin S., J. Thomas Hastings, and George F. Madaus. *Handbook on Formative and Summative Evaluation of Student Learning*. New York: McGraw-Hill Book Company, 1971.

Bruner, Jerome S. *The Process of Education*. Cambridge, Mass.: Harvard University Press, 1960.

Dewey, John. *The Child and the Curriculum*. Chicago: The University of Chicago Press, 1902.

————. *Democracy and Education*. New York: The Macmillan Company, 1916.

————. *How We Think*. Lexington, Mass.: D. C. Heath and Company, 1933.

————. *Experience and Education*. New York: The Macmillan Company, 1938.

Dressel, Paul L., et al. *Evaluation in Higher Education*. Boston: Houghton Mifflin Company, 1961.

Dressel, Paul L., and Lewis B. Mayhew. *General Education—Explorations in Evaluation*. Washington, D.C.: American Council on Education, 1954.

Ebel, Robert L. *Measuring Educational Achievement*. Englewood Cliffs, N.J.: Prentice-Hall, Inc., 1965.

French, Will, et al. *Behavioral Goals of General Education in High School*. New York: Russell Sage Foundation, 1957.

Grobman, Hulda. *Developmental Curriculum Projects: Decision Points and Processes*. Itasca, Ill.: F. E. Peacock, Publishers, Inc., 1970. Ch. 3.

Gronlund, Norman E. *Stating Behavioral Objectives for Classroom Instruction*. New York: The Macmillan Company, 1970.

Hofstadter, Richard. *Anti-intellectualism in American Life*. New York: Alfred A. Knopf, Inc., 1963.

Hullfish, H. Gordon, and Philip G. Smith. *Reflective Thinking: The Method of Education*. New York: Dodd, Mead & Company, 1961.

Husén, Torsten (ed.). *International Study of Achievement in Mathematics*, Vols. I and II. New York: John Wiley & Sons, 1967.

Janowitz, Morris. *Institution Building in Urban Education*. New York: Russell Sage Foundation, 1966.

Koestler, Arthur. *The Ghost in the Machine*. New York: The Macmillan Company, 1967.

Krathwohl, David R., Benjamin S. Bloom, and Bertram B. Masia. *Taxonomy of Educational Objectives, Handbook II: Affective Domain*. New York: David McKay Company, Inc., 1964.

Macdonald, James B. "Responsible Curriculum Development," Ch. 5 in Elliot W. Eisner (ed.). *Confronting Curriculum Reform*. Boston: Little, Brown and Company, 1971.

National Society for the Study of Education. *Educational Evaluation: New Roles, New Means*. Sixty-eighth Yearbook, Part II. Chicago: The University of Chicago Press, 1969.

Oliver, Donald W., and James P. Shaver. *Teaching Public Issues in High School*. Boston: Houghton Mifflin Company, 1966.

Piaget, Jean. *The Psychology of Intelligence* (1947), translated by M. Piercy and D. E. Berlyne. Paterson, N.J.: Littlefield, Adams, & Company, 1960.

Popham, W. James, et al. *Instructional Objectives*. Chicago: Rand McNally & Company, 1969.

Popham, W. James, and Eva L. Baker. *Systematic Instruction*. Englewood Cliffs, N.J.: Prentice-Hall, Inc., 1970.

Raths, Louis E., Merrill Harmin, and Sidney B. Simon. *Values and Teaching*. Columbus, Ohio: Charles E. Merrill Books, Inc., 1966.

Rich, John M. *Education and Human Values*. Reading, Mass.: Addison-Wesley Publishing Company, 1968.

Russell, James E. *Change and Challenge in American Education*. Boston: Houghton Mifflin Company, 1965.

Scriven, Michael. *The Methodology of Evaluation*. Chicago: Rand McNally & Company, 1967.

Silberman, Charles E. *Crisis in the Classroom*. New York: Random House, Inc., 1970.

Skinner, B. F. *The Technology of Teaching*. New York: Appleton-Century-Crofts, Inc., 1968.

––––––. *Beyond Freedom and Dignity*. New York: Alfred A. Knopf, Inc., 1971.

Taba, Hilda. *Curriculum Development—Theory and Practice*. New York: Harcourt Brace Jovanovich, Inc., 1962. Ch. 14.

Tyler, Ralph W. *Basic Principles of Curriculum and Instruction*. Chicago: The University of Chicago Press, 1950.

Watley, Donivan J., and Robert C. Nichols. *Career Decisions of Talented Youth: Trends Over the Past Decade*. Evanston, Ill.: National Merit Scholarship Corporation, 1969.

Whitehead, Alfred North. *The Aims of Education and Other Essays*. New York: The Macmillan Company, 1929.

Wilhelms, Fred T. (ed.). *Evaluation as Feedback and Guide*. Washington, D.C.: Association for Supervision and Curriculum Development, NEA, 1967.